D1395201

THE STRUGGLE FOR THE SOUL OF SCIENCE

KUHN
VS
POPPER

STEVE FULLER

REVOLUTIONS IN SCIENCE
Published by Icon Books UK

Published in the UK in 2003
by Icon Books Ltd., Grange Road,
Duxford, Cambridge CB2 4QF
E-mail: info@iconbooks.co.uk
www.iconbooks.co.uk

Published in Australia in 2003
by Allen & Unwin Pty. Ltd.,
PO Box 8500,
83 Alexander Street,
Crows Nest, NSW 2065

Sold in the UK, Europe, South Africa
and Asia by Faber and Faber Ltd.,
3 Queen Square, London WC1N 3AU
or their agents

Distributed in Canada by
Penguin Books Canada,
10 Alcorn Avenue, Suite 300,
Toronto, Ontario M4V 3B2

Distributed in the UK, Europe,
South Africa and Asia by
Macmillan Distribution Ltd.,
Houndmills, Basingstoke RG21 6XS

ISBN 1 84046 468 2

Series editor: Jon Turney

Originating editor: Simon Flynn

Typesetting by Hands Fotoset

Printed and bound in the UK by
Mackays of Chatham plc

CONTENTS

INTRODUCTION

One of the more poignant things my mother says is, 'I am not the person I set out to be.' This sentence should stick in your mind when you think about the principals in what turned out to be the most influential debate about science in the 20th century. By the end of their lives, less than a decade before this book is being written, Thomas Kuhn (1922–96) and Karl Popper (1902–94) were not who they set out to be.

Today it is hard to believe that a debate ever took place. *The Structure of Scientific Revolutions* by Thomas Kuhn – originally published in 1962 – has sold a million copies, has been translated into over twenty languages, and has remained for over 30 years one of the ten most cited academic works. The easiest way to start a discussion about science with people from varied backgrounds is by mentioning Kuhn. Usually the response is positive, even enthusiastic, except from those who still want to uphold 'falsifiability' as science's gold standard. These dissenters do not like Kuhn's picture of science as a collective enterprise beholden to 'paradigms'. They hark back to Karl Popper, who believed that at its best science epitomised humanity at its best. Ironically, this 'best' is simply the realisation that we can always do better. In practice, it meant that the best scientists always challenge what most people – even their fellow scientists – believe, however unpopular that may leave them.

It is puzzling, even from this brief description, why Kuhn is seen – as he invariably is – as a radical theorist of science, whereas Popper is remembered as a grumpy autocrat. They certainly did not intend their respective images. Kuhn started life as an earnest physicist who asked big questions that his discipline had recently rejected as too 'philosophical'. He never really managed to acquire the resources necessary for addressing those questions, and became more reticent as his views acquired notoriety and attracted criticism. In contrast, Popper began life as a socialist with a strong libertarian streak, who believed that science's critical gaze was crucial to social progress. However, over his lifetime, Popper rarely received the recognition he thought he deserved – and never tired of reminding everyone of it. His critical ideals increasingly took the form of hectoring and carping. In the pages that follow, we shall get behind these misleading images to their motivating ideas and contexts.

If Kuhn's intellectual horizons were warped by premature fame, Popper's were warped by fame overdue. Nevertheless, today the public understanding of science dwells in the space filled by these wounds, which are largely the product of a traumatic history over which neither Kuhn nor Popper had much control: two world wars and especially the Cold War. Although they disagreed on most things, they had no doubt that science was in worse shape in 1990 than in 1890. Admittedly, they expressed their dissatisfaction in rather extreme ways. Kuhn simply kept his counsel on the disposition of contemporary science, while Popper thundered against virtually every dominant tendency in the physical, biological and social sciences. Their students and emulators have followed suit and have been equally misunderstood.

This book is designed to recapture the full range of issues that separated these two self-styled defenders of science. Many of these issues plumb the depths of the Western psyche: What is the relationship between knowledge and power? Can science bring unity to knowledge? Can history bring meaning to life? At the same time, these issues are entangled in more secular concerns about economy and society, politics and war – most of which are still very much with us today. In that respect, I hope that this book will help to rekindle debates about matters that were not properly aired at the time Kuhn and Popper first raised them to public consciousness. While no one doubts that Kuhn has won the debate, I intend to question whether it has been for the better.

My own intellectual trajectory belies the nostrum that greater study of a phenomenon engenders greater sympathy for it. For me, to explain is most emphatically not to excuse. Like most others of my generation, I have been under Kuhn's spell. But gradually I wondered why the uptake of his radical-sounding ideas has eventuated in the timid understandings of science we find today. The answer, I submit, lies in the poor grasp we continue to have of the social implications of alternative regimes of knowledge production. Overriding concerns about rationality and progress in science as a whole, so characteristic of Popper and previous philosophers of science, have been replaced by more technical analyses of the relationship between evidence and inference in particular fields. The only remaining questions seem to be whether the appropriate 'techniques' are philosophical or sociological. Lost is an ongoing and wide-ranging discourse about the direction that should be given to a form of inquiry that could command universal assent.

Epistemology – the theory of knowledge – is now

more than ever preoccupied with face-saving exercises to shore up expertise, the elusive quest for what philosophers call 'credible testimony' and sociologists call, more brutally, 'boundary maintenance'. This is a project that Kuhn could understand. In contrast, when founding a field called 'social epistemology' fifteen years ago, I defined the social character of knowledge in terms of the need to bring order to an inherently divisive situation consisting of many self-interested and fallible agents. This is a project Popper could understand. However, most of those who nowadays call themselves social epistemologists are concerned with determining the spontaneous patterns of deference in a socially distributed knowledge system: Who should I believe? This pressing question is more likely to be answered by delegating than assuming responsibility for whatever informs one's actions. As students of political thought will appreciate, it is as if Kuhn's triumph over Popper has enabled social epistemologists to take the great leap backward: after all, who needs an explicit social contract for science, when science's own social relations constitute a natural aristocracy?

Popper's view that a non-scientist might criticise science for failing to abide by its own publicly avowed standards is rarely found inside academia today. For those who have inherited Kuhn's Cold

War belief that normal science is a bulwark in a volatile world, it comes as no surprise that philosophers today sooner criticise Creationists for violating evolutionary strictures than evolutionists for violating more general scientific norms – an activity for which Popper had been notorious. Even today's overheated turf battles that characterise the so-called Science Wars turn on little more than who is more properly immersed in the scientific practices under investigation: Does taking a few science courses measure up against spending a few months observing a laboratory? Kuhn deserves much of the credit – or perhaps blame – for dissipating what had been a genuine struggle for the soul of science into an endless series of competency tests.

In any case, unlike the other famous debate that Popper lost, the one recently recounted in the best-seller *Wittgenstein's Poker*, the outcome of his debate with Kuhn really mattered. With the defeat of Popper (and his followers), the normative structure of science drastically changed. Whereas actual scientific communities existed for Popper only as more or less corrupt versions of the scientific ideal, for Kuhn the scientific ideal is whatever has historically emerged as the dominant scientific communities. In the wake of Kuhn's victory, science has come to be justified more by its paradigmatic pedigree than by its progressive aspirations.

A few years ago I wrote a very controversial book about the origins and impacts of Kuhn's *Structure*. At the time, I did not have an opportunity to study Kuhn's archives. I now have, and I take a perverse pleasure in admitting that nothing I have read there causes me to revise my original critical evaluation – only to deepen it. The reader will acquire a good sense of my critique in the pages that follow. Since that time, two excellent intellectual histories related to the Popperian side of the story – by Hacohen and Kadvany – have been published. I refer the reader to the end of this book for the details. Once again, I would like to thank the secretary of Harvard College, the curators of the Harvard University Archives and the curators of the MIT Archives and Special Collections for their permission to examine the papers that I cite.

I would like to thank Jon Turney and Simon Flynn for giving me the opportunity to write for Icon Books, whose publishing philosophy I share. This book has been written in many locations over a short period. All of them have given me opportunities to present material from it. Here I acknowledge the Copenhagen Business School, Tokyo International Christian University, Tokyo Institute of Technology, Yogyakarta Center for

Cross-Cultural Studies (Indonesia), UCLA Center for Governance, University of New South Wales, and University of Warwick. In connection with these and other matters, I would like to thank Zainal Abidin, Thomas Basbøll, Lyn Brierley-Jones, Stefano Gattei, Stephanie Koerner, Susanne Lohmann, Yoichiro Murakami, Hideto Nakajima, Nicolas Rasmussen, George Reisch, Francis Remedios, Ziauddin Sardar and John Schuster. A special word of thanks goes to my long-suffering partner Stephanie Lawler, who has caused me to take the concept of responsibility more seriously than I would have otherwise. Finally, this book is dedicated to Ted McGuire, Department of the History and Philosophy of Science, University of Pittsburgh, who as my Ph.D. supervisor launched me on this strange and wondrous journey.

CHAPTER 1

IN SEARCH OF THE CAUSES
OF A NON-EVENT

The clash between Popper and Kuhn is not about a mere technical point in epistemology. It concerns our central intellectual values, and has implications not only for theoretical physics but also for the underdeveloped social sciences and even moral and political philosophy.

Imre Lakatos, 'Falsificationism and
the Methodology of Scientific
Research Programmes'

ARISTIDES BALTAS: *The way we have perceived things, which may be wrong, is that the big boom ... of the reception of Structure arrives after '65, more or less – when you had this London thing ...*
THOMAS KUHN: *I can't tell you that you are wrong, but I'm a little surprised at it; I would not have told the story that way ... I would not have thought that there was any particular burst in connection with '65.*

from Thomas Kuhn's last major interview
(1995), reprinted in *The Road since Structure*

The Kuhn–Popper debate, strictly speaking, refers to an encounter that took place at the former Bedford College, University of London on 13 July 1965, as part of the International Colloquium in the Philosophy of Science. It was designed to pit a relatively young theorist of science (Kuhn, aged 43) whose 1962 book, *The Structure of Scientific Revolutions*, was touted as the latest word from the United States, against a relatively old theorist of science (Popper, aged 63) whose seminal book, *The Logic of Scientific Discovery*, had been translated into English only in 1959, a quarter-century after it first appeared in German. Neither had been especially concerned with the other prior to 1965, though they had met briefly in 1950 when Popper gave the William James lectures at Harvard. After the London debate, the two never again significantly engaged with each other, either in person or in print, though both remained intellectually active for another three decades. So, then, why do most courses in scientific method today – regardless of specific disciplinary origin – continue to reserve a place for 'Kuhn vs Popper'?

There are two sides to this question. The first concerns how the debate managed to happen in the first place, given the tenuous link between a recently tenured historian of science (Kuhn) and a nearly retired philosopher of science (Popper). The second concerns how the debate managed to have such long-term significance, given that the parties themselves did virtually nothing to pursue their disagreements beyond the one encounter. This book is focused mainly on the second question, but something needs to be said about the first.

The debate's organiser was Imre Lakatos (1922–74), then Lecturer in Logic at the London School of Economics, where Popper presided as Professor. Lakatos staged the debate to pave the way for his own 'third way' between what he hoped would be seen as the extreme stances taken by Kuhn and Popper toward the constitution of the scientific enterprise. From Lakatos' standpoint (which was largely correct), Kuhn and Popper represented the authoritarian and libertarian poles of philosophical science policy. However, neither Kuhn nor Popper wanted this debate to look like a debate. Kuhn never believed in the value of formal confrontations, while Popper – who officially embraced them – would not agree to equal billing with the upstart Kuhn. But Popper did agree to chair a session in which Kuhn, Lakatos and Popper's most radical follower, Paul Feyerabend (1924–94), would try to map the conceptual ground covered between Kuhn and Popper. Since Kuhn's paper was already commissioned to appear in a Popper *Festschrift*, much of the sting of the encounter would be mitigated. In this context, Lakatos hoped to compare favourably with his sparring partner, Feyerabend, whose 'epistemological anarchism' combined the worst tendencies in Kuhn and Popper – or so Lakatos thought.

Unfortunately, neither Feyerabend nor Lakatos finished his paper on time, though the eventual fruits of their endeavours bore the marks of a long gestation. 'Consolations for the Specialist' turned out to be a written-up version of Feyerabend's unanswered correspondence with Kuhn, while 'Falsificationism and the Methodology of Scientific Research Programmes' was an annotated and more sophisticated version of Lakatos' undergraduate lectures. Both are included in the volume that Lakatos and his student, Alan Musgrave, finally published five years after the debate, the seminal *Criticism and the Growth of Knowledge*. However, at the time of the encounter, it seemed that Kuhn would be left alone to face Popper – and Kuhn himself was still working on his paper! The first line of defence was to have an eager and adept student familiar with *The Structure of Scientific Revolutions* to fill the available space. However, Kuhn, perhaps because of his own academic insecurities, refused to share the podium with the student, Jagdish Hattiangadi, who went on to chair Canada's most innovative philosophy department. Instead, Kuhn agreed to respond to Hattiangadi's mentor, John

Watkins, who relied on the student's notes and eventually succeeded to Popper's chair – which had been Lakatos' own lightly veiled ambition in the entire affair!

After the comedy of errors surrounding the non-event that was the Kuhn–Popper debate, matters really snowballed out of Lakatos' control. In the next five years, Kuhn so clearly trumped Popper in the court of public opinion that, after enjoying about fifteen years of focused attention, Lakatos' own views have now been relegated to a historical curiosity – a last-ditch effort to save some remnant of Popper against the Kuhnian onslaught. The irony here is especially cruel, since had Lakatos not staged the debate, it is unlikely that Kuhn and Popper would ever have been subject to such sustained comparison. Nevertheless, Lakatos correctly saw the disagreement between the two as being more profound than the mismatched nature of the original encounter might suggest. Lakatos, whose fondness for political imagery has yet to be taken with sufficient seriousness, was absolutely right about the deep difference in sensibility between the two protagonists. Kuhn was indeed authoritarian and Popper libertarian in their attitudes to science. This point has been largely lost, if not inverted, by those who regard 'Kuhn vs Popper' as a landmark in 20th-century philosophy of science.

This brings me to the second side of the question: the source of the debate's continuing significance. Kuhn and Popper tapped into long-simmering, deep-rooted disagreements that went well beyond the pages of their major works on science. Indeed, both can reasonably lay claim to having been seriously misinterpreted by friends and foes alike. The situation has not been helped by the standard presentation of the 'Kuhn–Popper debate' in textbooks on philosophy and the scientific method. In terms of scholastic affiliations, Popper is portrayed as objectivist, realist and positivist, while Kuhn appears as subjectivist, relativist and historicist. Popper is presented as the last defender of a unified conception of science closed under the authority of modern physics, whereas Kuhn looks like the apostle of scientific pluralism and methodological open-mindedness. When not completely false, these standard characterisations are too misleading to be helpful – in understanding either our protagonists or, for that matter, the nature of contemporary science.

To be sure, wilful simplification for the sake of clarity is philosophy's stock-in-trade. It reveals just how beholden the field's research frontier remains to its teaching function. Thus, philosophers – even the great ones – spend most of their time attacking straw opponents who fail to correspond to any actual precursor but who are no less vivid as phantom presences in student textbooks. By his own admission, Kuhn's understanding of logical positivism was almost entirely of this character. But so too was Popper's sense of his favourite foes Plato and Hegel. Sometimes behind such scholastic fodder that frames philosophical debate lie opponents who are not so different from each other after all. For example, a closer look at 'rationalists' like Descartes and 'empiricists' like Locke shows them to be much more alike than suited Kant's own purposes when he first distinguished the two theories of knowledge at the end of *The Critique of Pure Reason*. But sometimes the stereotype, for all its crudeness, *does* capture differences in sensibility that become deeper the more one looks. This is certainly the case with Popper and Kuhn.

Our investigation starts with a comparison of what Kuhn and Popper said and how they were received in their day. It soon becomes clear that these thinkers regarded the significance of science rather differently. Kuhn was tightly focused on science as a knowledge enterprise, whereas Popper invested science with symbolic import as the standard-bearer for critical rationality, a virtue in all walks of life. Although both Kuhn and Popper have been subject to widespread misinterpretation, Popper's followers understood the stakes sufficiently to be disturbed by Kuhn's emphasis on science's more authoritarian tendencies. I then examine the scientific, philosophical and political precedents for the Kuhn–Popper debate that enabled it to resonate long after the antagonists' one encounter. Here I stress the alienation of the philosophy of science from scientific practice, a situation common to both Kuhn and Popper. I argue that philosophers often uphold science's unrealised historic potential, which I identify with a 'Tory' approach to the writing of history.

I then turn to another, perhaps surprising, route to the deep structure of the Kuhn–Popper debate, namely, religion. It is easy to forget that both science and religion are preoccupied with justifying beliefs. Moreover, Christianity has been especially divided over whether the faith is better served by dogmatic or heretical attitudes toward Scripture. The Kuhn–Popper debate has been so polemical because it reintroduces this problem to science – after secular philosophers have tried to forget it. Yet, for all their concern with the fixing and changing of scientific beliefs, neither Kuhn nor Popper was very explicit about where these things happened in social space. Thus, I move on to the 'absent presence' of the university in their discussions.

The rest of the book is concerned with the more explicitly political dimensions of the Kuhn–Popper debate, especially as they bear on today's science and intellectual life more generally. Shortly before Popper debated Kuhn in London over the philosophy of the natural sciences, he had sparred with Theodor Adorno in Germany over the philosophy of the social sciences. This debate marked a watershed in the dissolution of what I call the 'rationalist left', the coalition of liberals and Marxists who defended a unified conception of science as a beacon of human progress. I explore this debate in some detail, as it too has been subject to considerable misunderstanding, the main beneficiaries of which have been the post-leftist postmodernists for whom Kuhn is a standard-bearer. But for his own part, Kuhn studiously avoided engagement with the political or even more broadly intellectual uptake of his work. In the final three chapters, I argue that Kuhn must be ultimately regarded as someone whose view of science and sense of himself were captive to the US Cold War context in which he flourished. My benchmark in this discussion is the controversy over Martin Heidegger's philosophical significance in light of revelations about his Nazi past. Adopting a Popperian perspective, I conclude that the career of Kuhn and the reception of his work manifest failures of intellectual responsibility on several levels, from which we may still hope to recover.

CHAPTER 2

KUHN AND POPPER: A CASE OF MISTAKEN IDENTITIES

One especially interesting aspect of [Lakatos' conference] *volume is that it provides a developed example of a minor culture clash ... Read as an example, it could be an object for study and analysis, providing concrete information concerning a type of developmental episode about which we know very little.*

Thomas Kuhn, 'Reflections on My Critics'

So who were Kuhn and Popper, and what did they say? Let us start with the book that provided the occasion for the London encounter. *The Structure of Scientific Revolutions* by Thomas Kuhn was the most influential book on the nature of science in the second half of the 20th century – and arguably, the entire 20th century. Nevertheless, a reminder of the book's contents immediately makes this fact rather surprising. *Structure* purports to provide a general account of scientific change in 200 non-technical, lightly referenced pages, in the manner of an extended encyclopaedia entry, as the book was in fact originally conceived.

Structure's thirteen chapters roughly track the phases of a science's life cycle, starting with its divisive pre-scientific roots in metaphysics, religion and politics. For Kuhn, science begins in earnest with the adoption of a 'paradigm', which means both an exemplary piece of research and the blueprint it provides for future research. In securing a paradigm, researchers agree to a common pattern of work and common standards for adjudicating their knowledge claims. Most actual science – what Kuhn calls 'normal science' – consists of little more than the technical work of fleshing out the paradigm's blueprint. Kuhn deliberately selects the phrase 'puzzle-solving' (as in crossword puzzles) over 'problem-solving' to underscore the con-strained nature of normal science. Thus, the Galilean image of the scientist as the heroic breaker of tradition is almost a complete myth, as far as Kuhn is concerned. Most scientists are narrowly trained specialists who try to work entirely within their paradigm until too many unsolved puzzles accumulate. Once the number of such 'anomalies' has reached a certain threshold, the paradigm is in 'crisis', and only then do scientists legitimately engage in wide-ranging normative discussions about the future direction of their field. A 'revolution' occurs when a viable alternative paradigm has been found. The revolution is relatively quick and irreversible. In practice, this means that an intergenerational shift occurs, whereby new scientific recruits are presented with a history that has been rewritten to make the new paradigm look like the logical outgrowth of all prior research in the field.

As this précis already suggests, the role of history is a running theme in *Structure*. Specifically, Kuhn highlights the tension between, on the one hand, the sort of heroic and progressive history that scientists must tell themselves, their students and the public to motivate the minutiae of normal science and, on the other hand, the actual history of science with all its diversions, complexities and imperfections. Kuhn treats these two histories as 'separate but equal', mainly because he believes that the secret of science's success – its principled pursuit of paradigmatic puzzles – would be undermined if scientists had the professional historian's demythologised sense of their history. After all, in the great scheme of things, most actual scientific work turns out to be inconsequential or indeterminately consequential. Thus, scientists need to see themselves as somehow, even if only vicariously, contributing to the completion of the world-picture presupposed by their paradigm. This raises *Structure*'s second running theme, namely, the means by which people become scientists. Here Kuhn relies on the cognitive psychology of his day to liken both the initial acquisition and any subsequent shift in paradigms to a conversion experience or 'Gestalt switch', whereby one comes to see the world in a systematically different way. These running themes in a book that clearly extols the conservative character of science led Popper and his followers to cast Kuhn as a fellow-traveller of religious and political indoctrinators.

But of course, this was not how *Structure* was read by most of its admirers – if they actually did read the book. For while Kuhn's examples are drawn almost exclusively from the physical sciences, these are the disciplines that have probably paid the *least* attention to *Structure*, even though Kuhn himself was qualified only in physics. Kuhn's admirers are to be found instead in the humanities and the social and biological sciences. Throughout his career, Kuhn claimed nothing but ignorance of these fields. Indeed, Kuhn identified his Eureka moment – when his theory of paradigms finally gelled – as occurring when he witnessed the vast difference in the way social and physical scientists conduct arguments. No matter how much physicists dis-agreed on the value of a particular piece of research, they could always agree on an exemplar against which to judge it. This was not possible in the social sciences, where any candidate exemplar (say, Marx, Durkheim, Keynes, Freud, Skinner, or nowadays Foucault) would also be a lightning rod for fundamental disagreements.

Nevertheless, Kuhn's admirers persisted in wrenching *Structure* from its original context and treating it as an all-purpose manual for converting one's lowly discipline into a full-fledged science. These wishful readings of *Structure* have been helped by its readers' innocence of any alternative accounts of the history of science – often including their own – with which to compare Kuhn's. The errors then only deepened. They ignored that the book was happily published by the philosophy of science establishment that Kuhn was held to have deposed. They ignored that Kuhn never talked about any science that was done after the 1920s, despite his professional qualifications in contemporary physics. They ignored that Kuhn, far from being a 'scientific revolutionary', argued that revolutions were only a last resort in science – indeed, an indication of just how fixated scientists tend to be on their paradigm that they have no regular procedure for considering fundamental changes in research direction.

Unlike Kuhn's *Structure*, no single work epitomises Popper's position. He was always a 'philosopher' in the grand sense, for whom science happened to be an apt vehicle for articulating his general world-view. At the time of the Kuhn–Popper debate, much was made of the recently translated *Logic of Scientific Discovery*. However, that book was a substantially expanded version of work that Popper had done in the 1920s and 30s as a young dissenter from the logical positivists in their European phase, when they existed in Vienna as the Ernst Mach Circle, or simply the 'Vienna Circle'. Since logical positivism today is associated with genuflection to scientific authority, it is important to see why someone with as heightened a critical sensibility as Popper would have found the movement attractive.

'Positivism' and 'sociology' were words coined by the same person, Auguste Comte (1798–1857), who believed that the growing secularisation of Europe required a new universal authority to replace the declining Catholic Church. That authority was to be found in the unification of the sciences, the final product of which would be an overarching science – sociology – that would draw on the resources of the other sciences to administer to society's needs. Comte's vision flourished largely outside the universities, which remained in clerical control. In the Anglophone world, his main advocate was John Stuart Mill (1806–73), who put a more democratic – perhaps Protestant – spin on

Comte's authoritarian vision by arguing that positivism could be used to rationalise public life by making standards of argument logically and empirically transparent. This had already been a policy advocated by Mill's godfather, Jeremy Bentham, the founder of utilitarianism. Afterwards, positivism took hold as an ideal in the more politically liberal parts of Europe, notably Austria.

The logical positivists of the Vienna Circle were single-minded in trying to design a language that would reveal the forms of evidence and inference underwriting knowledge claims in such a way that any ordinary citizen could decide whether to believe them. However, more than half a century after Mill, these 'neo-positivists' faced an uphill struggle from both a growing dispersion of scientific effort and a growing gap between expert and lay knowledge. As a confirmed socialist, Popper was very sympathetic to the positivist struggle to hold all knowledge claims accountable to a publicly accountable procedure. Popper's disagreement with the positivists is best captured in their respective attitudes toward the role of logical deduction in science. It was in this context that Popper formulated his so-called *falsifiability* principle, by which he claimed to 'demarcate' science from pseudo-science.

Popper disagreed with the positivists over what

logic is for. For positivists, logic bolstered scientific authority, whereas for Popper logic challenged it. Shorn of all philosophical significance, 'deductive logic' is simply the derivation of a particular conclusion from a universal premise. However, for over a century now, developments in the theory and methods of deduction have been cast in algebraic notation. This practice has tended to mask the profoundly different uses to which philosophers would put the notation. For the positivists, deduction demonstrates the coherence of a body of thought, specifically by showing how more general knowledge claims explain less general ones, each of which provide some degree of confirmation for the more general ones. For Popperians, deduction is mainly a tool for compelling scientists to test the consequences of their general knowledge claims in particular cases by issuing predictions that can be contradicted by the findings of empirical research. This is the falsifiability principle in a nutshell. Popper regarded it as much more than merely one of many uses for logic. He treated it as the core scientific ethic.

It follows that *any belief whatsoever* may be scientific or not, depending on whether or not one tries to falsify it, which is to say, to test the limits of its validity. From Popper's standpoint, what the positivists found interesting about deduction was merely the *post hoc* rationalisation of the research process, the sort of reconstructed logic of science that one finds, say, in philosophy lessons, science textbooks, but nowhere else. For his part, Kuhn accepted Popper's critique of positivism but could find little historical basis for falsifiability as a working ethic in science. But Popper's normative horizons were always more expansive than Kuhn's. Once Popper's philosophy of science is read alongside his political philosophy, it becomes clear that scientific inquiry and democratic politics are meant to be alternative expressions of what Popper called 'the open society'.

This resonant phrase refers to the title of the first book Popper published in English, *The Open Society and Its Enemies*. Written in a scholarly, often polemical but always accessible style, this 600-page monster was the product of Popper's exile as an Austrian Jew in New Zealand during World War II. The book's publication fortuitously coincided with the end of the war, when it played a formative role in public debates over the 'future of civilisation'. The open society is one whose members, like the citizens of classical Athens, treat openness to criticism and change as a personal ethic and a civic duty. Popper's book is a critical intellectual history of the fate of this ideal, as it first emerged from the quarrels of the pre-Socratic Greeks until it was suppressed by the first great authoritarian, Plato, who set a terrible precedent for the subsequent history of philosophy and politics. Plato's crime, according to Popper, was to have perverted the idea of progress. To be sure, Plato had both the good and bad versions of progress, but the bad version got the better of him and his followers. The good version envisages the goal of progress to be an ideal that we approximate through trial and error, but without ever assuming that each trial necessarily gets us closer to the ideal. The bad version of progress envisages that no matter the outcomes of our trials, we always end up closer to the ideal. This is the position that Popper demonised as 'historicism'. Historicism's cardinal sin – at both the philosophical and political levels – is its refusal to admit genuine error and hence the need to alter one's course of belief or action.

Popper found historicism lurking behind many seemingly unrelated positions: e.g. knowledge by induction, legitimation by tradition, salvation by Providence, evolution by natural selection, not to mention the proletarian revolution by historical materialism. As the Popperians read him, Kuhn also endorsed historicism as part of normal scientific training. But there is another subtext to *The Open Society* that tends to go unmentioned, though it becomes increasingly prominent, as Popper traverses the centuries to discuss the great German dialectician, G.W.F. Hegel (1770–1831), and contemporary developments relating to Marxism and fascism. Popper characterises the Biblical Jews as a closed society whose 'tribal' identity came more from whom they opposed than what they stood for. From that standpoint, Christianity's universalism represented an important step toward the open society. However, like Plato's position, it contained the seeds of historicism, which have become especially dangerous in the modern period as historicist visions of scientific progress are attached to secular versions of Providence. Here Hegel is made to stand for all the authoritarian movements on the right and the left that have exploited this tendency. In contrast, when Popper looked for a version of his falsificationist scientific ethic in political philosophy, he found it in the decidedly anti-historicist, existentialist Christianity of the 'Danish Socrates', Søren Kierkegaard (1813–55), whose works had been translated into German during Popper's youth.

However, Popper's scientific existentialism was given a distinctive spin in Britain, where Bertrand Russell anointed Popper his successor as knight errant of liberal and rationalist values. It is worth stressing both the philosophical and the political sides of Popper's assumption of Russell's mantle.

Russell and Popper shared an antipathy not only to authoritarian politics but also to philosophical professionalism. As they saw it, each had its own self-certifying way of evading responsibility for the consequences of its assertions – be it called 'reasons of state', 'common sense', or 'ordinary language'. This view had a profound effect on the post-war generation of British politicians on the Labour Party's social democratic wing, such as Anthony Crosland and Richard Crossman, who fought for greater social accountability in economic performance and political practice. Popper's 'open society' was taken to support government that decentralised its own power at the same time as it redistributed wealth. Not surprisingly, then, in the same year that he debated Kuhn, Popper was sounded out for a knighthood by representatives of Harold Wilson's Labour government. Popper accepted the honour two years later.

However, in 1965 both Kuhn's and Popper's views on *science* were probably known more by reputation than by readership. Once Popper's *Logic* was finally published in English in 1959, it was treated to a simplistic and bemused response, as often befalls works that are translated long after their original publication. Even positive reviews gave the impression that Popper was yesterday's man, an image that Lakatos' conference did nothing to dispel. Typical was the *Times Literary Supplement*: 'One cannot help feeling that if it had been translated as soon as it was originally published, philosophy in this country might have been saved some detours.' Popper's philosophy of science was read as either a slight weakening of positivist strictures – replacing verification with falsification as the logical basis of science – or a dispensable elaboration of his works on anti-authoritarian politics and social science, *The Open Society* and *The Poverty of Historicism*. Thus, Popper was made to appear a much more dogmatic defender of the scientific establishment than he ever was.

In contrast, Kuhn's relative obscurity served his reviewers' rhetorical purposes well. *Structure* received appreciatively critical reviews by those interested in reviving the fortunes of the American national philosophy, pragmatism, which had been eclipsed by the rise of logical positivism. The positivists were among several intellectual circles that, upon their escape from Nazi Germany, brought an unprecedented level of professionalism to American academia. Against this backdrop, Kuhn's focus on science as a mode of experience was credited with having reintroduced a 'human' dimension to science that had been the hallmark of pragmatism but was lost in the positivists' special- ised preoccupation with the logical structure of theories. Kuhn's reception was helped in this respect by young philosophers like Stanley Cavell and Dudley Shapere, who like Kuhn were trained at Harvard, the university whose faculty most self-consciously cultivated the idea of a distinctly American intellectual tradition, one which happened to coincide with that institution's initiatives. Unsurprisingly, this tendency was also promoted to a second-order preoccupation with 'forms of life' and 'communities of practice', which eventually became the central topic of Harvard philosophy. That Kuhn was even more specialised in his understanding of 'science' than the positivists – and certainly pragmatists like William James and John Dewey – seemed to elude the reviewers.

Kuhn's one previous book, *The Copernican Revolution*, was a sophisticated textbook whose lack of original scholarship failed to impress the Harvard committee that in 1956 had decided against granting Kuhn tenure. Such books, including ones with greater intellectual ambitions by Gerald Holton and I.B. Cohen, were staples of the General Education in Science programme in which Kuhn had taught. However, *The Copernican Revolution* was distinguished by its foreword, written by James Bryant Conant (1893–1978), President of Harvard (1933–53) and chief scientific administrator for the US atomic bomb project. In the Cold War, Conant was second only to his fellow Yankee Republican, MIT Vice-President Vannevar Bush, as an architect of US science policy. Whereas Bush was primarily focused on the future of scientific research (he was the mastermind behind the National Science Foundation), Conant planned for the education of potentially influential non-scientists in a period when public expectations of science were being exaggerated, both positively and negatively.

It was in this context that Kuhn, a physicist disillusioned by his experience in World War II, honed the ideas that became his second book, *Structure*. Indeed, Kuhn's first academic post was as Conant's teaching assistant in one of his general education courses. Although *The Copernican Revolution* dealt with events that transpired 400 years earlier, Conant felt compelled in his foreword to draw attention to the Cold War, especially the relationship between scientific autonomy and democratic America. Five years later, when Kuhn dedicated *Structure* to Conant, it became clear – at least to Lakatos and his London colleagues – that Kuhn had been anointed the official philosopher of science of the emerging military-industrial complex. After all, in World War II, Conant had helped to rescue the logical positivists, who by the start of the Cold War had become the philosophy establishment in the United States. Moreover, it was Conant who recommended Kuhn to the positivist editorial board that commissioned and published *Structure* as the final volume of their great American project, the International Encyclopedia of Unified Science.

CHAPTER 3

POPPERIAN SUSPICIONS AND KUHNIAN VINDICATION

When it repudiates a past paradigm, a scientific community simultaneously renounces, as a fit subject for professional scrutiny, most of the books and articles in which that paradigm had been embodied ... [The] result is a sometimes drastic distortion in the scientist's perception of his discipline's past. More than practitioners of other creative fields, he comes to see it as leading in a straight line to the discipline's present vantage. In short, he comes to see it as progress. No alternative is available to him while he remains in the field. Inevitably those remarks will suggest that the member of a mature scientific community is, like the typical character of Orwell's 1984, the victim of a history rewritten by the powers that be. Furthermore, that suggestion is not altogether inappropriate. There are losses as well as gains in scientific revolutions, and scientists tend to be peculiarly blind to the former.

Thomas Kuhn,
The Structure of Scientific Revolutions

Legend has it that while Popper liked to confess to the murder of logical positivism, Kuhn really did the dirty deed. In this tall tale, Popper is portrayed as a kind of renegade positivist, someone who tried to break away from the positivists' scholastic fixation on logic but did not quite succeed the way Kuhn did. To their credit, no Popperians were fooled by this story, especially since the relationship among the principals was rather more intimate. In particular, Rudolf Carnap (1891–1970), doyen of the logical positivists, was among the editors who agreed to publish *both* the original German edition of Popper's *Logic* and the first edition of Kuhn's *Structure*.

Seen from London in the 1960s, Kuhn retained the most objectionably conservative features of logical positivism, the very things against which Popper had revolted – only now in a less technically forbidding and more engagingly written form. Both Kuhn and the positivists assumed that science requires stable foundations for both legitimising and directing inquiry. But whereas the positivists aspired to completely universal foundations, covering all sciences for all times and places, Kuhn was satisfied with contingent foundations drawn from the actual history of science. Thus, instead of relying on the positivists' formal logic and neutral observation language, Kuhn proposed under the protean rubric of 'paradigm' the idea that scientific inquiry is anchored in an exemplar that researchers then use as a model for future investigations. As the Popperians saw it, Kuhn simply replaced the positivist search for timelessly true propositions with historically entrenched practices. Both were inherently uncritical and conformist.

Moreover, the Popperians suspected that Kuhn's peculiar, even duplicitous, attitude toward the history of science was designed to do double duty – to shore up science's noble image of autonomous inquiry in the face of its greater involvement in politics, the economy and societal regulation. Here lay James Bryant Conant's own invisible hand on Kuhn's work. In this respect, Conant and Kuhn continued the Platonic tradition of promulgating different truths according to mental preparation – the so-called *double truth doctrine* – as a means of stratifying and stabilising a pluralistic society. As Paul Feyerabend told Kuhn himself, the strategy amounted to 'ideology covered up as history'.

Kuhn may be known mainly for the swarm of buzzwords that *Structure* introduced to the general reader – paradigm, scientific revolution, incommensurability, Gestalt switch, normal science, exemplar, disciplinary matrix – but his ultimate significance lies in the attention he drew to the role of historical revisionism in the establishment of a new paradigm. For Kuhn, a paradigm succeeds by monopolising the means of intellectual reproduction, specifically, the terms in which the next generation learns about a past as a legacy they are entrusted to take forward. Kuhn astutely compared this process to the continually airbrushed historiography practised by the Ministry of Truth in George Orwell's *Nineteen Eighty-four*. Orwell rules not least in the canonical presentation of the Kuhn–Popper debate.

A distinguishing feature of Orwellian historiography is that events, ideas and people that not so long ago appeared progressive are now deemed reactionary – and vice versa – depending on what suits the ruling party. In a post-Kuhnian haze, we like to say that the 'context' has changed for making such evaluations. Kuhn himself is often quoted as claiming that when paradigms change, the world changes. Kuhn's dictum is then 'charitably' read as a dramatic way of saying that the world appears differently under the conceptual framework associated with a new paradigm. But this overlooks the essence of Kuhn's *Realpolitik* of science: scientific revolutions succeed not because the same people are persuaded of a new way of seeing things (*à la* Popper) but because different people's views start to count. It does not matter if a stubborn old scientist refuses to change her mind, since once the post-revolutionary paradigm has taken root, a young politically correct version will come to replace her. So, Kuhn's talk of 'world changes' should be taken literally, after all.

To be sure, for Kuhn, the ability to understand the world through two paradigms with radically different – or 'incommensurable' – assumptions, a skill he compared to bilingualism, is not restricted to historians of science who enjoy the benefit of hindsight. It is also a mental capacity present in such scientific revolutionaries as Galileo and Einstein. Kuhn's interesting and controversial point here is that very few scientists are intellectually bilingual because it is not part of their normal training. Consequently, the main propellant of revolutionary change in science is that subsequent generations are taught only the new and not the old paradigm. Scientists are not taught to be mentally flexible.

The revolutionary process may not happen overnight, but its implications are clear. Argumentation in science does more to sway uncommitted spectators, especially if they are young or newcomers to the field, than to change the minds of the scientific principals themselves. The sheer fact that newcomers have not yet personally invested in the old paradigm may be enough to make them open to a radical change in direction. From that perspective, matters of 'tradition', 'track record', 'accumulated wisdom' and 'presumption' are myths perpetuated in scientific textbooks to indoctrinate the young in the dominant paradigm. However, as Kuhn points out, these myths need to be reinvented after each scientific revolution; hence, the Orwellian turn.

Such is the 'genius' of inter-generational succession that Kuhn honoured under the name of the *Planck Effect*, named for the Nobel Prize-winning founder of quantum mechanics, Max Planck (1858–1947), who had a series of polemical exchanges on the future of German science with Ernst Mach (1838–1916) in the years leading up to World War I. As we shall shortly see, the tenor of their exchanges presaged the issues raised in the Kuhn–Popper debate. Among other things, Planck correctly predicted that Mach's anti-establishment scientific views would die with him because he lacked academically well-placed students to reproduce and extend his position. Mach's vanquished status is reflected in the fate of his admirers as *philosophers* of science, specifically the logical positivists – in whose number Popper may be included here. Kuhn's own 'genius' lay in concealing the brute biological character of the Planck Effect, whereby decisions about, say, whose students to hire constitute a second-order version of natural selection.

In contrast, Popper struggled throughout his career against the crypto-Darwinist tendency to turn risking an idea into risking one's life. No less than our sense of humanity hung in the balance. Popper tried to make good on the German idealist slogan that we rise above the animals when pursuing the life of the mind, for only then do our ideas truly die in our stead. While Popper granted that revolutionaries like Galileo and Einstein were more the exception than the rule in the history of science, he interpreted what Kuhn benignly called 'normal science' as a moral failure, not a successful adaptation strategy.

Unfortunately, 40 years later, Kuhn seems to have had the last laugh. The story of *Structure*'s reception in the philosophical community has been a tale of two halves, which together provide a striking confirmation of the Planck Effect. The first twenty years consisted of an array of negative responses, ranging from Popperian high dudgeon to more pedantic charges of ambiguity and inconsistency. In the last twenty years, however, a new generation has come to dominate the history, philosophy and sociology of science. They take *Structure* as the unproblematic foundation for its inquiries – as if the original criticisms had never been made. Certainly Kuhn never answered the criticisms, and the current generation of science studies practitioners is sufficiently beholden to *Structure* not to want to answer them. One thing must be said in Kuhn's behalf: he succeeded according to the terms set out by his own theory.

CHAPTER 4

WE'VE BEEN HERE BEFORE: THE PREHISTORY OF THE DEBATE

In recent years, however, it has become fairly clear that affluence may also be an obstacle [to progress in science]: *too many dollars may chase too few ideas … The danger is very real, and it is hardly necessary to enlarge upon it, but perhaps I may quote Eugene Wigner, one of the early heroes of quantum mechanics, who sadly remarks: 'The spirit of science has changed'.*

Karl Popper, 'The Rationality of
Scientific Revolutions'

[Kuhn's] *ideology of science could only give comfort to the most narrow-minded and the most conceited kind of specialism. It would tend to inhibit the advancement of knowledge. And it is bound to increase the anti-humanitarian tendencies which are such a disquieting feature of much of post-Newtonian science.*

Paul Feyerabend, 'Consolations for
the Specialist'

The series of exchanges alluded to in the last chapter between Max Planck and Ernst Mach anticipated the Kuhn–Popper debate in many respects. The paper trail launched by both sets of encounters defined the course of science in the 20th century. The Planck–Mach debate was prompted by the acknowledged success of the physical sciences in raising the unified Germany to global prominence within a single generation. By the time Kuhn and Popper met in London, over a half-century later, the balance of scientific power had shifted from the German to the English-speaking world, especially the United States. Between Planck–Mach and Kuhn–Popper came two world wars that sent mixed messages about the lessons to be learned from German science. In the end, much more of the German legacy was adopted than rejected – from people and ideas to work patterns and strategic goals. This was no less true in the meta-scientific arena where Kuhn and Popper fought.

Planck championed scientific professionalism, which for him meant that society should support the pursuit of science for its own sake. In contrast, Mach was a liberal activist with a spottier record as a professional scientist. He regarded himself as pro-science, but he also believed that society should support science only insofar as it promotes other human ends. The implications of this disagreement

43

ranged from the technical evaluation of scientific theories to the formulation of the research agenda and the institutionalisation of science as a school subject. It was popular at the time to cast the debate as turning on the existence of atoms, which Planck affirmed as the ground of physics' unique epistemic authority and Mach denied as a reification designed to protect the scientific establishment from public scrutiny. Faint echoes of the original richness of this debate may still be heard in today's scholastic quarrels between what philosophers call 'realism' (Planck) and 'instrumentalism' (Mach).

Kuhn and Popper resumed the exchange, but in a new key. Whereas Planck and Mach were practising physicists, Kuhn and Popper were merely more-or-less informed interpreters of physics. The terms of engagement had been transferred to a higher level of abstraction. What had been originally a debate in science policy now found itself in philosophy of science. This fact alone signalled that Planck had won the first debate. Science was no longer the preserve of rich amateurs (e.g. Darwin) or an adjunct of the liberal arts (e.g. Newton). It was now publicly recognised as a social force in its own right whose activities somehow manage to retain their autonomy while they transcend the walls of the university. If an argument were to be had, it would be over how to legitimate what scientists were already doing, not over whether they should be doing it.

But even granting Planck's point – that science should be pursued for its own sake – a new version of Mach's original problem suggested itself: Can scientists be trusted to uphold their own scientific ideals? Mach, always suspicious of the self-regarding character of scientific élites, found a new champion in Popper, who held that science is much too important to be left to scientific discretion. The growing authority of scientists in society offers too many opportunities for the corruption of science. Philosophers are thus needed to ensure that scientists remain true to the normative ideal, 'Science' with a capital 'S', a stern taskmaster who demands that scientists be critical of even their most cherished beliefs. From this impulse came Popper's falsifiability principle as the scientific ethic.

Kuhn's sensibility could not be more different. For him, an activity is not a proper science, unless the community of inquirers can set its own standards for recruiting colleagues and evaluating their work. Just as public oversight had no role in Planck's science policy, philosophical oversight cannot be found in Kuhn's theory of scientific change. One might think that such an élitist vision would have no place in today's world, where the costs and benefits of science loom as large as those of any other public policy. Yet, Kuhn managed to succeed simply by ignoring the issue, leaving his readers with the impression – or perhaps mis-impression – that, say, a multi-billion-dollar particle accelerator is nothing more than a big scientific playpen.

Popper and his followers were unique in seizing a glaring weakness in Kuhn's theory: Kuhnian normal science was a politically primitive social formation that combined qualities of the Mafia, a royal dynasty and a religious order. It lacked the sort of constitutional safeguards that we take for granted in modern democracies that regularly force politicians to be accountable to more people than just themselves. Scientists should be always trying to falsify their theories, just as people should be always *invited* to find fault in their governments and consider alternatives – and not simply wait until the government can no longer hide its mistakes. This notoriously led Popper and his students to be equal opportunity fault-finders across the natural and social sciences.

Nevertheless, Kuhn's political primitivism has been closer to that of Western national science policy-makers who, since the end of World War II, have presumed that self-organising bodies of scientists, roughly corresponding to academic disciplines, can determine the best researchers and research, and need change course only when they see fit. Moreover, once scientists have deemed that their knowledge has sufficiently matured, it can become the grounds for expertise and technology. Thus was legitimated the so-called 'linear model' for the conversion of 'basic' to 'applied' research, which was a staple of Cold War science policy. Such a strategy avoids difficult second-order questions about the relative merits of the knowledge produced by two distinct bodies of scientists: Should we fund more physics *or* more biology? What does each discipline contribute to our reasons for pursuing science as such? Silence on these matters is typically broken only during a fiscal crisis, when scientists are forced to operate within tight budgets. But policymakers see this as very much 'external' to the normal course of science policy.

Of course, like the most enduring monarchies, the scientific establishment continues to enjoy widespread public support on most matters, including the tinge of divine inspiration that has traditionally legitimated royalty. It might therefore be claimed that science already represents 'the will of the people', and hence requires no further philosophical schemes for democratisation. Here Popper's anti-majoritarian approach to democracy – what I would call his 'civic republican' sensibility –

comes to the fore. Many authoritarian regimes, especially the 20th-century fascist and communist ones, could also persuasively claim widespread popular support, at least at the outset and in relation to the available alternatives. For Popper, however, the normative problem posed by these regimes is that their performance is never put to a fair test. Kuhn suffers from the same defect: a paradigm is simply an irrefutable theory that becomes the basis for an irreversible policy.

Popper's pro-active strategy for challenging dominant scientific theories – including his critical attitude toward the histories that legitimate those theories – aims to render science as *game-like* as possible. The full import of this point has been rarely appreciated, mainly because it has not been taken literally, perhaps even by Popper himself. It means that rational decisions about science as a form of inquiry cannot be taken, unless two general conditions are met. First, tests cannot be biased toward the dominant theory. This is akin to ensuring that two opposing teams operate on a levelled playing field during a match, regardless of the differences in their prior track records. Second, the tests must not be burdened with concerns about the costs and benefits of their outcomes, especially in relation to the political and economic prospects of the scientists or their supporters. Allowing such considerations to influence the course of play would invite the equivalent of match-fixing.

Once these two conditions of science's game-like character are met, it becomes clear that the sense of 'progress' relevant to science is modelled on improved gamesmanship, as reflected in periodic changes in the game's rules, typically in response to tendencies that have emerged over several test-matches. Thus, a game progresses if its players' performance expectations rise.

It is easy to see how the gaming metaphor would make science continuous with philosophy, which has also become more sophisticated over time without achieving a final goal or even accumulating results. Nevertheless, the metaphor also reveals the remoteness of this normative ideal of science from actual scientific practice. Consider three points of divergence:

1. The track records of competing theories normally count in evaluating a scientific experiment, thereby placing a much greater burden on the upstart to produce an outcome that exceeds the expectations of the orthodoxy.
2. An anticipated low benefit-to-cost ratio of overturning an established theory is treated as grounds for dismissing an upstart's formal challenge, especially when the relevant

experiment would require large public expenditures.

3. While scientific norms have palpably changed over time, these changes have rarely been the result of formal legislation; rather, they have reflected a statistical drift toward imitating the practice of acknowledged winners.

These three non-game-like features of science have served to impede any global evaluation of the state of organised inquiry in relation to its putative goals. One is simply encouraged to follow the inertial tendencies of tradition because it would seem that too much would be placed at risk to do otherwise. Thus, from a strict Popperian standpoint, contemporary 'Big Science' is a regressive form of organised inquiry. This is *not* to deny that science may succeed as an economic productivity multiplier or, for that matter, a Keynesian job-creation scheme for the surplus of over-educated people. Science may serve several social functions at once, but rarely all equally well. Indeed, science's success as a source of societal governance and economic growth may have been at the cost of its progress as a form of inquiry.

If the history of politics has made any progress at all, it has been by the introduction of periodic elections for fixed terms of office. This institution, associated with the civic republican roots of democracy, routinely forced societies to think about what they have done and what they want to do next, especially given the available alternatives. Of course, the citizenry may decide to retain the incumbent, but elections force this decision to be explicitly justified and not simply be allowed to proceed uncritically, as in the case of hereditary succession. The genius of democracy lies not in the content of political party proposals or even their policy track record, but in the capacity of politicians to face the scrutiny of the electorate. On the one hand, citizens must always be alive to what might be lost by continuing to give consent to the powers that be. On the other, politicians who change their policies when they fail to produce the desired results display an acceptance of responsibility for which they should be praised.

In contrast, as science has acquired more secular power, it has tended toward the self-perpetuation of existing regimes, as dominant research programmes are pursued by default, a situation that the sociologist Robert Merton has dignified as the 'principle of cumulative advantage'. Kuhn and Merton, both Harvard products of the Conant years, were kindred spirits. They saw science as mainly about those few who rise above the rest and constitute themselves as a self-perpetuating community. 'Self-stratifying' more than 'self-organising' describes the situation. Recalling the political logic of George Orwell's *Animal Farm*, all scientists working in the same paradigm are equal, but some are more equal than others. These are the 'peers' whose opinions always seem to matter in the 'peer review processes' used to fund and evaluate scientific research. The only sense in which Kuhnian scientists dictate the terms of their own inquiry is that they all agree to abide by the decisions taken by their élite peers. This, in turn, provides a united front of legitimacy to the larger society. It should then come as no surprise that Kuhn's only interest in the sociology of science lay in the acculturation of novices into a scientific paradigm, since thereafter the novice's mind is set to plough the deep but narrow furrow laid down by her senior colleagues as normal science.

Thus, Popper had a rather distinctive take on the universal character of scientific rationality. He took seriously both that science aspires to universal knowledge and that scientists – our representatives in this project – are inherently flawed and biased agents. The result was to make science as game-like and democratic as possible. But it is equally worth noting the intrinsic connection Popper saw between irrationalism and élitism, which marks him as a kind of Hegelian *malgré lui*. Given Popper's own aversion to Hegel's authoritarian tendencies, it was left to Lakatos to make the connection explicit: the idea that a social group – be it a culture or a science – has proprietary rights over a domain of reality is 'irrational' because of the asymmetry between what is purported objectively and subjectively about the domain in question: knowledge is alleged to be objectively true without being subjectively true – that is, a minority has exclusive access to what is supposed to be applicable to everyone. In short, what is universally true is not also universally *known* as true. Under the circumstances, knowledge becomes an instrument for concentrating, rather than diffusing, power: a means of domination rather than liberation.

In science, this sense of 'irrationality' is most evident in its slavish adherence to *track record* – what Popper demonised as 'induction' – whereby the sheer fact that a particular discovery was made under the aegis of a particular theory is used as the basis for claiming that *only* upholders of that theory have proper access to that discovery. The logical positivists tried to address the problem of track record by proposing a neutral observation language into which all knowledge claims could be translated. Accordingly, healthy sense organs and rudimentary calculative skills are all you need to judge such claims for yourself. You need not be committed to a particular research programme, or even formally trained in it. Popper differed from his positivist cousins only in his insistence that this language must be itself revisable in light of future developments in science and society.

Nevertheless, the fact that both learned academics and ordinary folks do not normally question the devolution of allegedly universal forms of knowledge to specific experts testifies to Plato's lingering influence. As a result, intellectual discrimination continues to function as a relatively non-coercive vehicle for social control. In this respect, Kuhn is the latest rider on Plato's wave. While neither Kuhn nor Popper would care to deny that a specific paradigm may dominate the understanding of a particular slice of reality at a particular time, they differ over whether it should be treated as a source of stability (Kuhn) or a problem to be overcome (Popper). Authoritarian interpretations of Hegel rest on the former view, while Lakatos tried to recover a more liberal interpretation of Hegel that spoke to the latter. Here a set of analogies proves useful: what Popper demonised as 'historicism' relates to history's openness to the future as monopoly capitalism relates to the free market – or alternatively, as Kuhn's winner-takes-all view of scientific paradigms relates to a public good conception of scientific knowledge whereby innovations are distributed as widely as possible.

Thus, Kuhn and Popper embody both 'pluralist' and 'universalist' attitudes toward scientific inquiry, though each turns the two terms to opposite effect. Kuhn's pluralism is a reluctant outcome compelled by his brand of universalism, whereas Popper eagerly embraced pluralism as a means for realising his brand of universalism. For Kuhn, a science is always dominated by one paradigm that its members pursue religiously until it runs up against the limits of its puzzle-solving capabilities. Pluralism then emerges in the form of increasingly specialised domains of inquiry, each dominated by its own paradigm. In contrast, for Popper pluralism is, at least ideally, intrinsic to the day-to-day conduct of scientific inquiry, as scientists are encouraged to proliferate alternative hypotheses that then face stiff cross-examination by standards that command universal assent. To be sure, Popperians have tended to stress – more than Popper himself – that scientists may rationally continue to pursue hypotheses after they have been falsified but *only* in the recognition of what it would take to change the minds of fellow inquirers.

Textbook caricatures of Kuhn and Popper tend to

resort to facile binaries like 'relativist/realist' to capture the two sides of their argument. If one philosophical binary does capture what is at stake, it is a distinction originally drawn by the Austrian phenomenologist Franz Brentano, who divided consciousness into two parts: a 'transcendent' object of consciousness that serves an external standard against which the 'immanent' content of our consciousness is evaluated. If we substitute 'content of consciousness' with 'the dominant beliefs of the community of inquirers', then Popper held that truth is always 'transcendent' of the community of inquirers, whereas for Kuhn truth is always 'immanent' in the community. If Kuhn located truth within a scientific paradigm, Popper found it in a 'meta-language' into which the knowledge claims of the paradigm may be translated and evaluated.

On the broadest philosophical canvas, one that simultaneously addresses the concerns of science, religion and politics, Kuhn and Popper represent two radically different ways of specifying the ends of inquiry: What drives our understanding of reality? Where is the truth to be found? Kuhn would have us look to the dominant paradigms, the beliefs and actions of those who have come to be certified as knowers. It is ultimately a backward-looking standard, one based on entitlement through survival. For his part, Popper proposed a more forward-looking perspective based on what enables us to think that our knowledge and actions are always subject to improvement.

CHAPTER 5

DIALECTICS AS THE PULSE
OF SCIENTIFIC PROGRESS

Popper used to say that science is philosophy by more exact means. He had in mind the kind of critical philosophy that proceeds by dialectical engagement, pitting one hypothesis against a counter-hypothesis over a commonly disputed matter. This procedure goes back to the Athenian law courts, the local model for Socrates' own brand of questioning, which was eventually institutional-ised as an academic practice with scholastic disputation and, with the 19th-century reinvention of the university, the German dialectical tradition, culminating in Hegel and Marx. However, this lineage was always haunted by the spectre of scepticism, which takes consistently applied critical inquiry to the point of self-destruction. It was with this lineage in mind that Lakatos invited the leading historian of scepticism, Richard Popkin, to give the opening speech at the conference that featured the Kuhn–Popper debate.

Lakatos was alive to this strain in Popper's thought because of his own doctoral research into the 19th-century roots of modern mathematical proof theory, which was published posthumously in 1976 as *Proofs and Refutations: The Logic of Mathematical Discovery*. For Popper and Lakatos, as well as the 19th-century mathematicians, deduction was used more to uncover and eliminate errors in arguments than to justify entire systems of reasoning, as a logical positivist might have expected. In this Popperian sense, 'to make a discovery' is *not* to generate a new, self-certifying experience of reality – what science popularisers call a 'Eureka experience' – but to recognise a limit in our current understanding of reality. However, Lakatos found Popper's exploitation of this negative side of the discovery process much too radical. Indeed, in debate with Kuhn, Popper refashioned Trotsky's 'permanent revolutionary' stance as his own. However, for Lakatos this was tantamount to nihilism, since every new theory is born refuted, not yet having had the chance to pursue its distinctive course of inquiry long enough to see how it truly differs from its competitors.

Lakatos understood well the nihilistic side of dialectics. Though trained mainly in mathematics, he had been a research assistant of the great Marxist philosopher György Lukacs (1885–1971) in his native Hungary. For three decades, Lukacs was Stalin's most eloquent apologist. Today he is more mercifully remembered for his early scholarship that led to the recovery of Marx's debt to Hegel. Lukacs showed that Marx adapted Hegel's sense of the 'cunning of reason' in history – to explain how capitalism would become a victim of its success, as the relentless pursuit of profit would alienate those in its pursuit, thereby creating a permanent underclass that would eventually rise up against capitalism's diminishingly few beneficiaries. Lukacs held that Hegel gave Marx a fine appreciation for the invisible hand's perverse sense of humour. Indeed, one might say that Lakatos himself became the butt of one of Hegel's jokes.

Lakatos realised that science, mathematics included, has made progress – in a way that philosophy has not – by its *selective* encouragement and appropriation of criticism, or in terms that could have come from that master German dialectician, Hegel, criticism applied critically to itself. In other words, criticism is productive only under certain conditions – for example, *not* in a research programme's early stages. Kuhn implicitly understood this point much better than Popper. But at the same time, Lakatos could not tolerate Kuhn's conservative complacency, which went to the other extreme of permitting criticism only once a standing paradigm had already run into so many difficulties that it had entered a state of 'crisis'.

Lakatos believed he had improved on Popper's account by showing how – at least in mathematical inquiry – the discovery of error is followed by something more than the simple removal of the falsified theory. Rather, in the process that Lakatos called 'lemma incorporation', a counter-example to a theory is retransmitted as a boundary condition for applying a successor version of the theory. Thus, error elimination is made into a genuinely collective learning experience, whereby a *prima facie* negative episode in the theory's history becomes a feature of its logical structure.

Moreover, from a pedagogical standpoint, this process is better seen as *dialectical* than strictly deductive. Dialectics lays bare patterns of reasoning that are normally mystified by mathematicians' appeals to the 'intuitiveness' of a proof's axioms and lemmas. The social, indeed rhetorical, dimension of mathematical inquiry is therefore finally exposed. Lakatos would have us focus more on how one from among several competing sets of axioms came to be selected than on how, once selected, this set manages to entail a set of conclusions.

Why does Lakatos' preoccupation with dialectics matter in the Kuhn–Popper debate? The answer is encapsulated in what analytic philosophers call the *underdetermination thesis* – the idea that any body of evidence can be explained by any number of mutually incompatible theories. In that case, theory choice is 'underdetermined' by the evidence. Whether the evidence base is the fossil record or the Holy Bible, it is easy to see how many conflicting interpretations can be generated, hence providing intuitive support for the thesis. Nevertheless, this is not how science has been officially portrayed, at least since Newton claimed to have 'deduced from phenomena' his laws of motion. But if the underdetermination thesis is true, how does one choose between theories that purport to save the same range of phenomena?

Pierre Duhem (1861–1916) is normally credited with the underdetermination thesis. He believed that the question uniquely arose in his own discipline, physics, because of the laboratory conditions in which experiments are normally conducted. In that case, how are the field's artificially generated results to be judged in relation to alternative accounts of the natural world? As a Catholic living in France's Third Republic, with its clear separation of church and state, Duhem turned to divine illumination for guidance – but only because of the epistemic limits of physical inquiry implied by the underdetermination thesis. Fifty years later, Harvard logician Willard Quine (1908–2000) universalised and secularised Duhem's original thesis. Quine replaced God with whatever theory had the best track record, a kind of evolutionary naturalism that upheld a conservative presumption in the conduct of inquiry. This was the solution that Kuhn popularised and both Popper and his students opposed with their dialectical conception of inquiry.

According to the Popperians, a research pro-gramme's track record is a rational reconstruction that selectively draws from history for self-serving purposes. Kuhn could hardly disagree. However, very unlike Kuhn, the Popperians concluded that these histories require at least as much criticism as the scientific theories legitimated by them. Indeed, they would resolve underdetermination by shifting the locus of action in science from explaining what is already known to predicting what has yet to be known. This move presupposes that the conditions of dialectical engagement are in place:

1. Two or more theories, whatever their funda-mental disagreements, must recognise each other as holding contradictory views on the disposition of some unknown matter: they must find something worth contesting.
2. They must also agree on a procedure for resolv-ing the contest, what Popper following Francis Bacon called a 'crucial experiment', the out-come of which is binding on the contestants.

Lakatos differed from Popper in allowing not only the same scientists but also the same scientific theories to join battle in the future, though defenders of a defeated theory would carry a liability into the next engagement. Two points are striking about the dialectical resolution to under-determination.

First, it draws attention to what economists call the 'opportunity costs' of theory choice. In other words, when designing the test case for rival theories, scientists are forced to think about theory choice as simultaneously involving the rejection of one or more other theories. This situation naturally invites later reflections about whether the selection of one theory over another had come at too high a price. Kuhn's view of science disallowed precisely these considerations because a new paradigm rewrites its history to make it appear as though its ascendancy was an eventuality – not a deliberate choice with consequences that may have been unforeseen at the time, regretted now, yet still reversible in the future.

Second, the dialectical resolution shows that theory choice is rarely, if ever, *forced* on scientists. Rather, scientists usually must themselves under-take the regular contestation of theories. Here the followers of Kuhn and Popper were in agreement, but drew opposing conclusions. Kuhnians – much more than Kuhn himself – concluded that science has rather little to do with theory choice, since incommensurable research programmes can be conducted *in tandem* indefinitely and, more importantly, individual scientists can give each programme its due without feeling compelled to decide between them. Ian Hacking has perhaps most aggressively pursued this line from the philosophical side, arguing that science is ultimately about the accumulation of phenomena that remain robust in the face of passing theoretical fads. Recent historians and sociologists of science have continued the epistemic demotion of scientific theories by casting them as flexible rhetorics that can be deployed to suit the occasion.

For Popperians, this casual attitude toward theory choice – or boundless theoretical pluralism – amounts to intellectual irresponsibility. At the very least, it fails to distinguish the scientist's responsibility for testing the limits of theories from the technician's capacity for indefinitely extending the application of theories.

A favourite Popperian example here is the 1,500-year life-span of Ptolemaic astronomy, which presupposed an Earth-centred universe. It lasted so long because it was treated largely as an off-the-shelf tool that could be used for astrological and navigational purposes alongside other theories and practices whose metaphysical and epistemological assumptions contradicted its own. There was no felt need for achieving a larger synthesis that would reconcile the fundamental differences between the various bodies of knowledge, as each was conceptually and empirically adequate to its own slice of reality. Of course, this all began to change in the late 16th century, when Galileo promoted Copernicus' Sun-based astronomy from a computational variant to a substantive challenge to Ptolemy's system.

What we call the 'modern', and distinctly Western, sensibility emerged as people tried to organise the conduct of the sciences in light of second-order considerations of what might be common to all the sciences. The result was a Galilean zeal for spotting latent contradictions between bodies of knowledge, the pretext for eliminating the social, linguistic and practical barriers to their proper integration into one system of thought. Popper promoted a version of this strategy in his attack on the 'myth of the framework', the Kuhnian idea that the presence of incommensurable theories rendered any explicit normative comparison so difficult that one simply had to wait for history to take its course, as individuals come to adopt one or another theory for their own reasons. In contrast, Popper argued that if the incommensurable theories are truly scientific, they aspire to universality, which means that there will be cases that they have yet to explain or predict. These cases may then serve as relatively neutral ground for designing a crucial experiment to decide amongst the theories.

In many respects, the postmodern condition associated with Kuhn's ascendancy marks a return to a *pre-modern* sensibility. What is often called 'relativism' – be it in praise or condemnation – is simply the ancient attitude, perhaps most clearly defended by Aristotle, that all knowledge must be adequate to its objects. Ethnographic sociologists now speak of 'context sensitivity' and cognitive psychologists of 'domain specificity' to mean much the same thing. While it may be possible to derive some abstract categorical principles (or 'meta-physics') from the various forms of knowledge, those principles are treated simply as objects in their own right with no expectation that they will shape the conduct of the first-order inquiries from which they were abstracted. This aspect of the history of Western thought follows a course similar to that of the great Eastern intellectual cultures of China and India, none of which ever managed to acquire the dynamism associated with modern Western science.

· CHAPTER 6 ·

A PARTING SHOT AT THE MISUNDERSTANDING

Kuhn's ideas are interesting but, alas, they are much too vague to give rise to anything but lots of hot air. Never before has the literature on the philosophy of science been invaded by so many creeps and incompetents. Kuhn encourages people who have no idea why a stone falls to the ground to talk with assurance about the scientific method. Now I have no objection to incompetence but I do object when incompetence is accompanied by boredom and self-righteousness.

Paul Feyerabend, 'How to Defend
Society against Science'

So, Popper was a democrat concerned with science as a form of dynamic inquiry and Kuhn an élitist focused on science as a stabilising social practice. Nevertheless, they normally appear with these qualities in reverse. How can this be? We have already seen that the texts of both thinkers are normally read so out of context that important background assumptions are systematically misunderstood. Consider one final example: what both thinkers made – and are thought to have made – of the received view that the physical sciences are superior to the social sciences because they are better at predicting and controlling the aspects of reality that they study.

On the one hand, Kuhn is read by his admirers as having levelled, or 'relativised', the status difference between the natural and social sciences by omitting any reference to the received positivist view from his account of scientific paradigms. For Kuhn, science is simply good at solving its self-defined problems, whose purely technical nature led him to dub them 'puzzles'. But far from demoting the physical sciences, Kuhn was actually trying – as a latter-day Plato might – to insulate them from responsibility for real world effects, entanglement in which has historically prevented the social and biological sciences from taking full control of their inquiries. For Kuhn, these secular entanglements explain the failure of these fields to become proper sciences.

On the other hand, Popper's detractors read him as endorsing the received view and hence treating the social sciences as uniformly inferior to the physical sciences. But this is false too. Popper championed what he called 'piecemeal social engineering', but this meant placing science's capacities for prediction and control in the service of checking social policies. Applications of science must thus be treated as reversible experiments, not unconditional mandates. In this respect, the word 'piecemeal' is unfortunate because it suggests that only *minor* improvements are possible. Unlike Kuhn, Popper's instinct was to extend the laboratory to society at large, not shelter it from political contamination. If Popper was 'scientistic' or 'positivistic', it was in precisely this sense: he wanted society to be reorganised so that it could be as genuinely experimental in its policies as a laboratory science is in its hypotheses. Moreover, the level of resolve needed to test one's policies in this fashion by no means corresponds to disciplinary affiliation or status. Social scientists are just as capable as physical scientists of rising to the challenge – or not, as the case may be.

A contemporary target common to both Kuhn and Popper was the idea of 'planned science' associated with the totalitarian regimes of Nazi Germany and the Soviet Union – but equally present among Stalin's admirers in Western Europe, ranging from humanists like Jean-Paul Sartre to scientists like John Desmond Bernal, not to mention US populists inspired by Franklin Roosevelt's New Deal. For all of them, science was ultimately the most efficient instrument for expediting social progress. However, Kuhn and Popper differed on where they thought planned science went wrong.

Consider the scientific scandal and economic disaster associated with Stalin's agricultural minister, T.D. Lysenko (1898–1976), who applied so-called Marxist genetics to grow wheat in the Soviet Union. Lysenko's theory had been based on Jean-Baptiste Lamarck's epistemically discredited – but ideologically attractive – view that traits acquired by one generation of organism can be transmitted genetically to the next generation. For Kuhn, Lysenko's problem was that he applied a form of knowledge that had yet to mature within an established scientific paradigm. For Popper, the problem lay rather in Lysenko's ability to escape acknowledging error once his agricultural policy had clearly failed. Had the Soviet Union been an open society, Popper would have permitted Lysenko a run for his money, whereas Kuhn still would not have, given the low esteem in which the relevant experts held Lysenko's science.

There is a large lesson to be learned from the systematic misunderstanding of Kuhn and Popper, thinkers so close to our own time: *Even if ideas and arguments should be evaluated independently of their origins, we must still first learn about those origins, in order to ensure that our evaluation is indeed independent of them.* The only thing worse than accepting or rejecting an idea because we know about its originator is doing so because we know nothing of the originator. Ignorance may appear in two positive guises. Both are due to the surface clarity of relatively contemporary texts, which effectively discourages any probing of their sources: on the one hand, we may read our own assumptions into the textual interstices; on the other, we may unwittingly take on board the text's assumptions. In short, either our minds colonise theirs or theirs ours. In both cases, the distinction between the positions of interpreter and interpreted is dissolved, and hence a necessary condition for critical distance is lost.

For Lakatos' old mentor, György Lukacs, the 'destruction of reason' came precisely from this failure to specify a standard of judgement that is independent of what is being judged, as that makes it impossible for the historically situated character of reason to be recognised, criticised, and corrected. Interestingly, Lukacs' original target in these remarks was American pragmatism as the ideology of what he recognised as the emerging hegemonic power of the Cold War. I shall show in the last three chapters of this book that it is possible to appreciate Lukacs' point here even without wearing his distinctly Red-tinted spectacles.

· CHAPTER 7 ·

WHY PHILOSOPHERS GET NO RESPECT FROM SCIENTISTS

How can a mere philosopher devise criteria distinguishing between good and bad science, knowing it is an inutterable mystic secret of the Royal Society?

Imre Lakatos, 'Lecture One on the Scientific Method' (1973)

The most striking feature of the history of the philosophy of science is the inverse relationship between the philosophical and the scientific significance of the people talked about. Even the very greatest scientists, such as Galileo, Newton, Maxwell and Einstein, tend to be treated as no more than passable philosophers of science. Sometimes others in that scientific league, most notably Charles Darwin, are relegated to polite philosophical silence. This curious feature first becomes noticeable when examining periods when 'natural philosopher' is used as an expression to cover both people who, by our lights, are scientists and philosophers. For example, 17th-century natural philosophers are nowadays divided into 'scientists' such as Galileo, Boyle and Newton, and 'philosophers' such as Descartes, Hobbes and Leibniz. The people we now call 'philosophers' are basically the natural philosophers on the losing side of the battles that we now call 'scientific'.

This embarrassing tendency becomes more pronounced as we get closer to the present. The major moments in the philosophy of science are defined by such notables of the 'long 19th century' as William Whewell, John Stuart Mill, Ernst Mach, Pierre Duhem and Henri Poincaré. All were recognised as scientists who engaged in major philosophical disputes with one another, other philosophers and other scientists. However, all turn out to have been scientific losers – often rather spectacular ones, as, say, the last cultured despisers of atomism and relativity. Indeed, sometimes opposing sides of a philosophical dispute may be united in scientific error. For example, Whewell and Mill battled over whether scientific knowledge is built from, respectively, the top down (i.e. deductively) or from the bottom up (i.e. inductively). Should science be a distinct profession requiring university training (Whewell) or an integral part of citizen education in a liberal democracy (Mill)? Nevertheless, both Whewell and Mill were in agreement that their contemporary

Darwin's theory of natural selection had failed to advance science's quest for a unified account of nature. This is the sort of complaint one might expect today from proponents of 'Intelligent Design Theory', the scientific version of Creationism.

Moreover, matters hardly improve upon turning to the 'professional' philosophers of science who emerge from logical positivism in the 20th century. The leading positivist, Rudolf Carnap, originally wanted to revive the classical philosophical task of unifying the sciences in his home discipline of physics. He had been impressed by Einstein's pencil-and-paper reconceptualisation of space and time. It reinforced a normative ideal, also common to Popper and Kuhn, that science is simply philosophy by more exact means. Unfortunately, Carnap's fellow physicists failed to see the need for any more conceptual grounding than what was already allowing physics to pose and solve interesting empirical problems. Thus, they rejected Carnap's dissertation proposal. However, philosophy, a field that had been in continual decline in German academia since Hegel's death in 1831, was only too glad to approve it. In heroic retrospect, the logical positivists appear as the last light of reason in the darkening philosophical landscape of Weimar Germany that eventuated in the rise of Hitler. Rarely is it added that they fell into this role after having been cast out from the organised science of their day.

Moreover, Carnap was profoundly disappointed by the ease with which, less than a decade after Einstein proposed the special theory of relativity, the German physics community fell into line with the practitioners of the epistemologically inferior science of chemistry to support the Kaiser's cause in World War I. In reaction, Carnap set a precedent that would sharply distinguish logical positivism from most previous pro-science movements: he attempted to justify physical knowledge without making any reference to its worldly applications. This is a precedent that Kuhn would follow. Carnap's model was mathematics' success in declaring disciplinary independence from physics and engineering in the 19th century by rediscovering its ancient Euclidean roots in deductive proof theory – the subject of Lakatos' doctoral research. Here Carnap had been influenced by his old teacher Gottlob Frege, whose arcane *Begriffschrift* ('concept writing') had been championed as 'symbolic logic' by Bertrand Russell and Carnap's fellow World War I veteran, Ludwig Wittgenstein, a self-loathing engineer who was heir to Austria's leading steel-making family. In the inter-war years, Wittgenstein intermittently attended the Vienna Circle meetings in which logical positivism's tenets were crystallised.

But the complete alienation of philosophy of science from mainstream science was best epitomised in the training of Karl Popper, who was nearly a dozen years younger than Carnap. He hovered in the periphery of the Vienna Circle, as he worked on a doctorate in educational psychology, a subject that officially aimed to make science easier to assimilate, not criticise. Popper's own original interest in the field, however, was inspired by children's resistance to novelty, or in the Kierkegaardian terms that Karl Jaspers had popularised among psychologists, 'anxiety toward the unknown'. However, Popper soon became equally disillusioned by Vienna's socialist educational authorities, who were keen on force-feeding students with reformist dogmas that were themselves never subjected to scientific scrutiny.

In the middle third of the 20th century, when logical positivism and the Popperian heresy reached their institutional peak in the English-speaking world, practising scientists accorded them little more than polite notice, even when they seemed to be making epistemological and ontological claims of grave import. For example, the American pragmatist philosopher who made the most successful transition to positivism, Ernest Nagel (1901–85), worried about the fate of science, if physical causation dissolved into indeterminacy at the quantum level of reality. For him, so-called quantum indeterminacy simply reified our remaining ignorance about micro-physical causation. Popper was more sanguine about this prospect, as he pursued the hypothesis that physical determinism is false. He proposed instead that reality consists of objective proba-bilities, or 'propensities'.

Neither Nagel's nor Popper's concerns led to the collapse, or even the reorientation, of physics. Rather, like other related foundational matters, they were simply cordoned off from physics' day-to-day empirical work. After all, physicists gain the respect of their peers by designing clever experi-ments whose results can be captured by elegant mathematical formalisms, all the while remaining agnostic about the metaphysical significance of their inquiries. This is what makes physics a specialised science, as opposed to a total ideology. It is also none other than Kuhnian normal science, which, in the case of quantum physics, continues apace – that is, until the funding runs out for its main instrument, the particle accelerator. Mean-while, physicists who show a keen interest in foundational questions are easily labelled 'has beens' and 'also rans' in the scientific sweepstakes. Even Nobel Prize winners are treated as overgrown children feasting on their intellectual dessert after having supped on the gruel of normal science. Such are the consolations of philosophy!

Perhaps I am focusing unfairly on the lack of impact that the positivists have had on the physics agenda. Subtle readers of the history of science know that positivism was always a 'made for export' philosophy. In other words, positivists have wanted to spread what they took to be the secret of physics' scientific success to the more backward disciplines. To be sure, the 'secret' varied over the history of positivism, but its social function remained largely the same. To imagine what positivism looks like to a physicist, consider how the zeal of a missionary or an imperialist appears to an enlightened believer or citizen at home: what causes the domestic market to cringe may just impress the overseas market.

Unfortunately, the positivist call for unity failed to impress biology, the science whose practitioners most clearly realised that it was in need of unification. However, this was not from lack of trying. The logical positivists declared biology a protoscience still mired in the metaphysical dispute between 'mechanism' and 'vitalism', which turned on whether life could be exhaustively explained by mechanical processes. Some positivists, focused on the molecular basis of genes, held that biology would be eventually reducible to physics. Others, focused on the morphological structure of organisms, proposed that biology would itself become the science to which sciences of the mind and society would be reduced. Although the former project no longer attracts much philosophical interest and the latter has been periodically fashionable (first as cybernetics, now as complexity theory), neither captured the actual strategy by which biology consolidated as the science we know today.

Instead, practising biologists followed the lead of the Russian Orthodox Christian, US-based geneticist Theodosius Dobzhansky (1900–75), whose 1937 book, *Genetics and the Origins of Species*, argued that biology could achieve an intra-disciplinary unification – what is now known as the Neo-Darwinian synthesis – without either subordinating itself to physics or lording over the human sciences. As Dobzhansky saw it, the main obstacle to biology's scientific autonomy was that natural selection appeared to be purely destructive and wasteful, leaving only a trail of extinct species and unrealised genetic potential in its wake. However, Dobzhansky argued, natural selection is not a uniform force that beats genetic variation into adaptive submission. Rather, it moves diffusely, placing specific environmental pressures on particular gene pools. Thus, natural selection reveals a creative side, akin to an 'invisible hand', that permits the survival of chance mutations in local settings that over time may transform entire populations of organisms.

Dobzhansky's co-operative vision of the relationship between genetics and natural history was rather unlike the traditional antagonism between the two fields that positivist philosophers, including Popper, continued to foster. The flavour of this conflict is captured in the schism between 'quantitative' and 'qualitative' methods that continues to plague the social sciences.

Geneticists are akin to experimental psychologists and mathematical economists who study humans under abstract conditions that enable maximum generalisation across environments. Researchers in this category have typically had a reformist policy bent, be it in agriculture or welfare, where the capacity for prediction and control is at a premium. In contrast, Darwin's original constituency, natural historians and ecologists, are like the field ethnographers and archival historians who aim to understand humans as products of unique environments. These researchers tend to adopt a more protective attitude toward the phenomena they study that sometimes verges on romanticism. Popper accused biologists in this category of the dreaded vice of 'historicism', as evolutionary theory appears to deal only in series of one-off events that could be retrospectively explained but never subject to testable predictions. In part, Popper was trying to make room for human agency, but the long-term beneficiaries of his critique have been, of course, anti-evolutionists seeking a place for divine agency.

A fitting conclusion to the philosophy of science's chequered history in relation to biology is the case of Kuhn, whose root-metaphor of scientific change as an endless cycle of normal and revolutionary phases was indebted to the model of biological change that the theory of natural selection decisively defeated in the 20th century. This is the so-called 'catastrophist' model introduced by the French Catholic palaeontologist Georges Cuvier (1769–1832), who interpreted the geological stratification of the fossil record as evidence for God's special creation and periodic replacement of the natural order. This view was exported to the US by Louis Agassiz (1807–73), the staunch anti-Darwinist who founded Harvard's comparative zoology museum, most recently home to such *malgré lui* critics of Neo-Darwnism as Richard Lewontin and Stephen Jay Gould. In the first half of the 20th century, Agassiz' anti-selectionist thinking migrated to the Harvard Medical School, where it was championed by the biochemist Lawrence J. Henderson (1878–1942), an early theorist of homeostasis and devotee of the anthropic principle, the perennially popular Aristotelian idea that the universe has been designed so as to be especially hospitable to human life.

Henderson occupies a special place in our story because he was largely responsible for making James Bryant Conant the first scientist to be president of Harvard University. As an avid reader of the Neo-Machiavellian sociologist Vilfredo Pareto, Henderson suggested to Conant the value of consciously cultivating an élite entrusted with preserving excellence in the face of external threat, notably Communism. The fruits of this advice were Harvard's Society of Fellows (where Conant and Kuhn consolidated their relationship) and Harvard's first history of science courses, which Henderson taught as part of general education. Uniting Henderson's practical and theoretical enthusiasms was the idea that each 'organic form' (interpreted liberally to include animal species, human societies – basically any complex carbon-based physical system) has its own pattern of development that it maintains, except in extreme cases, against external environmental pressures. Henderson turns out to be the common intellectual ancestor of three distinctive Harvard products of the second half of the 20th century: Talcott Parsons' structural-functionalist sociology, Stephen Jay Gould's punctuated equilibrium theory of organic change, and of course, Kuhn's theory of scientific change.

· CHAPTER 8 ·

SO, WHY ARE PHILOSOPHERS OF SCIENCE PRO-SCIENCE?

Given their penchant for being on the wrong side of history, why have philosophers of science been so keen to present themselves and their history as *pro*-science? Under the circumstances, one might reasonably expect that theirs would be a history of resentment, perhaps of genius spurned or suppressed. Yet, if anything, philosophers of science nowadays are much more explicitly philosophers *for* science than they used to be. They no longer defend, as Popper did, an ideal conception of science that would call into question much of what scientists normally do. Instead, philosophers relate to practising scientists as *underlabourers*, a term John Locke coined to characterise his own relationship to his friend Isaac Newton, the scientific 'master builder'. As underlabourer, Locke's job was to clear the rubbish in the way of the master builder's work. By analogy, the philosopher of science would clarify the conceptual foundations of the dominant scientific paradigms and defend them from attack. In terms of Plato's *Republic*, underlabourers belong to the class of Guardians, not Philosopher-Kings-in-training.

Kuhn was the crucial figure in this transition. Unlike the positivists and the Popperians, Kuhn did not postulate an end to science other than what satisfied the constraints laid down by the dominant paradigms. Thus, post-Kuhnians have come to accept scientists' working assumptions at face value, including the counter-intuitive implication that reality consists of many distinct worlds, each roughly corresponding to a scientific discipline. For example, whereas Lakatos had called on historians, philosophers and sociologists to master the technical details of contemporary science so as not to depend on scientists' own *ex cathedra* pronouncements about the merits of their research programmes, Kuhn's progeny master such details in order to impress scientists that they are sufficiently competent to be taken seriously at all. Kuhn's reduction of the ends of science to the trajectories already being pursued by particular sciences has now inspired two generations of philosophers to believe that they should be taking their normative marching orders from the sciences they philosophise about, and hence do not question them unless the scientists themselves have done so first.

At work here is not the scientific humiliation of philosophy but a relatively unnoticed legacy of

Cold War science policy – namely, the self-alienation of 'autonomous science'. In Plato's Academy, the pursuit of pure inquiry had been justified in terms of the mental discipline it provided for statecraft. According to Plato, a consequence of being focused on the ideal for many years would be a resolve to do what is right, even when it is unpopular. What Plato had not envisaged was that this fixation on the ideal would become an end in itself, which would then enable the work of the pure inquirers – mathematicians, philosophers, computer programmers, physicists – to be inserted unproblematically into military strategy and other governance schemes that were decided without their consent. That is, the Cold War social conditions underwriting the autonomy of science encouraged the scientist to function less as a free agent who aims to transcend boundaries than a cognitive module who operates within strict parameters. For those Central European émigrés who had experienced multiple regimes of science policy in their lifetime – Popper, Feyerabend and Lakatos included – this perversion of the Platonic programme was epitomised in Kuhn's valorisation of 'normal science', which locates the collective genius of science in its occasional ability to eke out innovation from a very narrow set of epistemic constraints. Today's philosophical underlabourers recreate this Kuhnian situation in their own relationship with scientists. It is less 'meta-science' than 'infra-science'.

In understanding how this heads-down 'organisational man' approach to science and the philosophy of science could come to be associated with a pro-science attitude, the role of warfare should not be underestimated. Kuhn and Popper's two main followers, Lakatos and Feyerabend, were born within two years of each other and served in World War II. Kuhn jammed German radar signals in East Anglia, applying the principles for which his Ph.D. supervisor would eventually win the Nobel Prize in physics. Feyerabend, who became best known for recommending 'anything goes' as science policy, dutifully flew planes for the Nazi Luftwaffe. For his part, as a young Communist, Lakatos joined the underground anti-Nazi resistance in his native Hungary. Like the logical positivists and Popper, all three were inspired by Einstein as the exemplar of science as natural philosophy by more exact means. However, World War II made it clear to all of them (and others – including Stephen Toulmin, Derek de Solla Price, Gerald Holton and John Ziman – who are now regarded as the founding fathers of the field called 'history and philosophy of science') that science's material conditions had diverted its mission from pure inquiry. Exceptionally disappointing was that physics 'scaled up' to accommodate the war effort without ever returning to its pre-war dimensions.

Kuhn responded to this situation much as the logical positivists had, namely, by never formally acknowledging the technological dimension of modern science, where science most naturally interfaces with our pre-scientific understanding of reality. Even when writing about scientific experiments, his focus remained fixed on the role of experiments in generating data, solving puzzles or testing theories – not on their material character as, say, an economist concerned with 'externalities' would treat experiments. In particular, he made a point of *not* asking whether the instruments used in experiments were inspired and/or applied in a military-industrial setting outside the experimental context.

From a psychiatric standpoint, the accounts of science put forward by the logical positivists and Kuhn (and perhaps even Popper) were 'reaction formations' in response to traumas that had dealt severe blows to their normative ideals of science. The traumas were, respectively, the 20th century's two world wars. In response, they promoted excessively idealised visions of science that were the opposite of the tendencies they rejected in the science of their day. For Kuhn, the ultimate corruption of the spirit by matter – or science by technology – had been epitomised by the involvement of the founders of modern particle physics in the US and German atomic bomb projects. The theorists of the ultimate constituents of matter and energy were also the designers of the ultimate weapons of mass destruction.

The differences between Kuhn and his positivist forebears lie in their specific reaction formations. Carnap and his fellow logical positivists retreated to mathematical formalism, while Kuhn and most of the current generation of science studies practitioners have had recourse to historiographical purism. The clearest symptom of this purism is a studied refusal to involve present-day judgements in accounts of past science. Thus, one tells the history entirely from the standpoint of the original agents, without passing judgement on the long-term significance of their actions. Indeed, for Kuhn, a proper understanding of a science's significance is possible only once its major disputes have been resolved, and the historian arrives on the scene as a spectator, not a participant. Kuhn philosophised this reaction formation as the *incommensurability thesis*. While this thesis has helped to undermine the sorts of triumphalist histories that scientists have told to raise funds and exert influence, it has carried an important cost: historical understanding would seem to require the abandonment of one's own world-view and hence one's responsibility for the events recounted. However, as we shall now see, the Popperians have been much less escapist in their appeal to history.

CHAPTER 9

THE RETURN OF THE REPRESSED: PHILOSOPHERS AS TORY HISTORIANS OF SCIENCE

One must realise that one's opponent, even if lagging badly behind, may still stage a comeback. There is never anything inevitable about the triumph of a [scientific research] *programme. There is also never anything inevitable about its defeat.*

Imre Lakatos, 'History of Science and Its Rational Reconstructions'

It would seem that the history of the philosophy of science has been one of endless disappointment, a graveyard for failed scientists and scientific ideas. However, there is a deeper lesson here. It is a version of Nietzsche's amplification of Hegel's master–servant dialectic to explain the origins of morality. Nietzsche argued that, starting with the Egyptian captivity of the Jews, morality has been the most effective revenge that the losers in history have had over the winners. The losers basically intimidate the winners into treating them well and perhaps even adopting some of their practices, out of fear of what an omnipotent deity friendly to the losers might do to the winners in the afterlife.

Similarly, the history of the philosophy of science is about scientists on the losing side of first-order disputes who acquire epistemic leverage by ascending to the second-order of inquiry, namely, the ideals that should guide the conduct of science. This explains the schizoid attitude of practising scientists, who are at once dismissive of philosophers' substantive scientific views, while they remain uneasy about whether their own research practices are sufficiently rational, objective, etc. However little their own practice conforms to philosophical ideals of inquiry, scientists feel compelled to justify it in those sanctified terms. Thus, science's own eternal return of the repressed helps to explain the confused legacy of the philosophy of science.

Unfortunately, this peculiar feature of the philosophy of science is lost amid blanket postmodernist attacks on 'master narratives', including ones where mastery occurs in the afterlife or the indefinitely deferred future. Master narratives are historical accounts of history that presuppose an active universal subject – one with whom the author happens to identify – who overcomes a series of obstacles to reach full self-realisation. This plot outline is common to the invisible hand of

Divine Providence in the Christian salvation story, the philosophical histories of progress recounted in the Enlightenment, the path of the world-historic spirit charted by Hegel, and the scientific theories of dialectical materialism and evolutionary naturalism inspired by Marx and Darwin. The style in which these histories are typically written is often called *Whig history*, named after the victors of the 17th-century English Civil War, who wrote of the conflict as one they were bound to win as defenders of liberty.

In the third quarter of the 19th century, once the modern natural sciences began to drive out natural philosophy and, more importantly, natural theology from pride of place in the universities, popular histories of science started to be written in the Whiggish mode. They are still largely written this way today, as witnessed by the continuing tendency of popularisers to pit the scientific worldview against some 'force of darkness' like religion, politics, literary criticism, or even common sense. Moreover, these Whig histories not only edify the general reader; the scientific respectability of their authors also testifies to the role of these histories in edifying practising scientists whose spirits would flag if they realised just how prone the actual history of science has been to contingency and ambivalence. Again we see Kuhn's nod to Orwell:

the rather technical and tedious work of normal science requires that scientists be in full control of their own historiography, continually rewriting it to keep their comrades motivated that they are indeed pushing back the frontiers of human ignorance.

At the same time, however, Kuhn paved the way for the postmodern critique of Whig history by calling for two 'separate but equal' historiographies of science – an airbrushed, inspirational one for scientists (and the general public) and a confusing but more accurate one for historians. Kuhn accepted this version of the double-truth doctrine as a Faustian bargain: scientists live a noble lie in public view, while historians cultivate the truth in the relative obscurity of their professional societies. We tend to fixate on the positive side of the bargain, namely, that Kuhn enabled history of science to be written by people with 'proper' historical training and not simply self-serving scientists who use history to influence contemporary debates. Unfortunately overlooked is that Kuhn purchased the autonomy of history of science precisely by condemning historians to irrelevance with respect to the contemporary scientific scene.

Postmodernists have rarely adhered to Kuhn's historiographical segregationism. Thus, in the ongoing Science Wars, cultural studies scholars (allegedly) try to demystify the natural sciences' claims to epistemic authority. In response to Whiggish tales of inevitable progress that suppress divergence and disagreement, they advance a plurality of parallel 'subaltern' accounts that aim to undermine science's narrative finality. It was exactly this sort of hostile engagement that made Kuhn suspicious, and sometimes even disparaging, of the entire field of science studies, despite his own status as its mythical progenitor.

But even if Kuhn's postmodernist admirers failed to meet the master's strict segregationism, they still kept to Kuhn's dualistic vision of the history of science. But is there a missing third way? Yes. It is the attitude toward history exemplified by Popper and his followers. They have not been afraid to proffer master narratives. However, instead of Whiggish tales of vindication, these are tales told by history's losers, specifically those dispossessed of a common legacy, the Whig's litigious sibling, as it were. In deference to the monarchist party vanquished by the Whigs, *Tory history* is the name given to this third way overlooked by both Kuhn and the postmodernists.

To the Tory mind, the actual history of science has produced sub-optimal outcomes, a source of continual disappointment at opportunities lost and potential unrealised in a story for which the narrator considers herself at least partly responsible; hence, her criticism is always a form of self-criticism. The ancient Greek paradigm of Tory history, Thucydides, was himself an Athenian general who went down to defeat early in the war that would eventually bring down Athens itself. Lakatos notoriously signalled the Tory sensibility in the philosophy of science by placing the normatively desirable course of history in the main body of his own text, while relegating the actual history to the footnotes. Such a posture irritated Kuhn, who was keen to let the history speak for itself, and has befuddled postmodernists, who generally expect the voice of resistance to come from a victim of the power structure, not a disinherited member of the élite.

Clearly, both Whigs and Tories have treated the past less as foreign lands for professional historians to colonise than as raw material out of which the present has been constructed for better or worse – which is to say, legitimately or illegitimately. In the Cold War era, Whig histories loomed large in the competing accounts of the Global March of Capitalism and Communism, where the one is portrayed as a temporary obstacle to be overcome before the triumph of the other. But Tory histories were in evidence as well.

The Tory counterpart of Communist triumphalism was Leon Trotsky's account of the Soviet Union's failure to launch a worldwide 'permanent revolution'. In the case of Capitalist triumphalism, the Tory sensibility was represented by the sociologist C. Wright Mills, who inspired American campus radicals in the 1960s by arguing that the United States had betrayed its own liberal democratic values by concentrating power in the military-industrial complex. Not surprisingly, Trotsky and Mills were considered traitors in their respective lands. For they were losers without being victims. Consequently, there was always the chance that they would return to reclaim their legacy.

Here it is worth mentioning the 'scientific' provenance of the Tory image of the 'return of the repressed', which fuelled the imaginations of not only Hegel and Nietzsche but also Ernst Mach and Sigmund Freud – as well as the Popperians, especially Lakatos. It goes back to the idea that Nature promotes *atavisms*, that is, throwbacks to supposedly extinct life-forms that nevertheless manage to survive in a second incarnation. Contrary to popular views of evolution as consisting of an irreversible sequence of endlessly progressive species, the presence of atavisms suggested that what might be otherwise seen as Nature's drafts on the blueprint of life are in fact conserved in the 'germ plasm' (or 'gene pool', as we would now say) awaiting propitious environments for their full realisation.

By analogy, starting in the 1880s, Mach, an arch atavist, collected together two centuries' worth of discarded philosophical objections to Newtonian mechanics. While this struck Max Planck and the physics establishment of the day as irrelevant antiquarianism, within a generation it served to inspire the revolutions associated with relativity theory and quantum indeterminacy. A similar preoccupation with historical atavism is evident in the Popperian discussion of 'Kuhn Loss', named for Kuhn's belief that a consequence of any scientific revolution is that some phenomena that had been encompassed by the old paradigm are lost by the new one, perhaps to be picked up by a paradigm in another field or simply left to wallow in a pre-scientific state. For Kuhn, such a 'loss' enables the new paradigm to acquire a sense of focus and progress lacking in the old one. But for Lakatos and Feyerabend, the lessons were more equivocal. Indeed, Feyerabend went so far as to mount a spirited defence of Aristotle's unified inquiry into the natural ends of motion, which drifted out of physics into biology and psychology, ultimately to disappear altogether from scientific view.

· CHAPTER 10 ·

THE RELIGIOUS UNCONSCIOUS OF THE DEBATE

My suggestion is, then, that Kuhn sees the scientific community on the analogy of a religious community and sees science as the scientist's religion. If that is so, one can perhaps see why he elevates Normal Science above Extraordinary Science; for Extraordinary Science corresponds, on the religious side, to a period of crisis and schism, confusion and despair, to a spiritual catastrophe.

John Watkins, 'Against "Normal Science"'

Belief *may be a regrettably unavoidable biological weakness to be kept under the control of criticism: but commitment is for Popper an outright crime.*

Imre Lakatos, 'Methodology of Scientific Research Programmes'

The very idea of a 'religious unconscious' to the Kuhn–Popper debate seems absurd. After all, our two antagonists scrupulously confined their attention to examining disciplines that at least claimed scientific status. At a personal level, both were secular Jews who did not exhibit any noticeable tendencies toward pietism or mysticism. Indeed, both of their accounts of science were so devoid of any overarching sense of purpose that they were continually plagued by charges of incoherence for failing to specify any ultimate end – say, the unification of all knowledge or the explanation of the cosmic plan – towards which science might be heading. Given that Kuhn and Popper saw themselves as positively disposed toward what each called 'science', this would seem to be a serious shortcoming. Nevertheless, they agreed that the sense in which science makes 'progress' has nothing to do with its ability to perfect the human condition, achieve absolute truth, or otherwise replace the Christian salvation story. In this respect, Kuhn and Popper appear to be even less religious than that other historically oriented secular Jew, Karl Marx.

However, as so often happens, appearances deceive. It turns out that religious conversion is Kuhn's model for the paradigm switch that occurs during a scientific revolution. Moreover, the analogy between a scientific discipline and a religious order had already been developed as a self-styled 'post-critical' philosophy by one of Kuhn's influences, the Catholic chemist Michael Polanyi (1891–1976). Polanyi was largely responsible for shifting the Anglophone public image of scientists in the 1950s from heroic individuals like Galileo and Darwin who tried to change the world to a more anonymous community of specialists focused on cultivating their craft. This monkish view of scientists, which Kuhn popularised in the following decade as 'normal science', was designed to protect the autonomy of science from policy-makers in both the Capitalist West and the Communist East who, during the Cold War, were keen on converting science into means for larger political ends. The tell-tale sign of this monastic turn in Polanyi and Kuhn is that the entire sociology of science is reduced to the process of training initiates for a life of total commitment to their paradigm, by virtue of which their judgement will go largely unquestioned in the larger society and questioned only on technical matters within their own community.

Despite his own steadfast support for the autonomy of scientific inquiry, Popper found the 'heads-down' approach of the monastic model abhorrent. For him, belief, let alone unconditional commitment, mis-characterised scientific claims to knowledge. Popper would rather have them treated as hypotheses that one explicitly decides to undertake, with the understanding that they will be subject to strenuous tests and, should these be failed, swift rejection: in short, a policy of 'conjectures and refutations'. Here, Popper was decisively influenced by two theorists of religion: the sociologist Max Weber (1864–1920) and the philosopher Henri Bergson (1859–1941).

Shortly after Germany's defeat in World War I, Weber made a pair of famous speeches on politics and science as vocations. There he distinguished between the *ethics of conviction* and the *ethics of responsibility*, in part to distinguish Marxism as a political movement and a scientific research programme, but also as an implicit critique of Germany's prosecution of the war. As politicians, Marxists (he was thinking of Lenin) are convinced that they already know the truth, which emboldens them to ignore the immediate consequences of their actions. But as scientists, Marxists realise that their access to the truth is partial, and thus propose policies in a more responsible, experimental fashion, withdrawing and revising them once they have clearly failed. Instead of science becoming more politicised, as many of his colleagues suggested, Weber believed that politics should become more 'scientised' *in the precise sense of adopting the ethics of responsibility*. Unfortunately, Weber's message has been often misread as an endorsement of the technocratic devolution of politics, when in fact he was trying to revive the original idealist vision of the German civil service under Wilhelm von Humboldt (about whom more in chapter 12). In any case, Weber probably provides the clearest source for Popper's falsificationism.

Popper was inspired to characterise science as the 'open society' by Bergson's last major work, *The Two Sources of Religion and Morality* (1932), where the phrase first appears. In Bergson's original terms, the closed society follows the Catholic, Hindu and Platonic practice of using degrees of knowledge and ignorance to stratify and stabilise the populace, while the open society follows the prophet who seeks to recover humanity's original connection to God by breaking through the layers of mythology, superstition and institutionalised dogma. For Bergson, the history of religion is marked by phases of institutional consolidation and reformation: for every Catholicism, there is Protestantism; for every Hinduism, Buddhism; for every Kuhn, Popper.

To appreciate what the open society as a religious orientation might mean, we may start with Popper's life-long fascination with the form of republican democracy that constituted the Athenian civil religion, and then move to consider Christianity's preoccupation with the nature of belief, which over the last century and a half has come to be secularised as the 'problems of knowledge' with which epistemologists are most familiar.

At various points in Western history – and ours seems to be one of them – classical Athens has been condemned as a democracy of élite males supported on the backs of women and slaves. Nevertheless, the Athenian political economy provided a unique environment for the cultivation of civic virtue. Because a secure income from local property was a prerequisite for citizenship, Athens expected its citizens to be unafraid to speak their minds. Indeed, failing to speak was worse than failing to persuade. The two failures resembled, respectively, cowardice and defeat in battle. One could return from defeat to fight another day, but cowardice was sometimes punished with 'ostracism', or expulsion from the field of engagement. But worst of all was what the Greeks called *stasis*, a semantically rich word that covered everything from intransigence to capriciousness in the conduct of public affairs. Common to these cases is that the public interest is held hostage to self-interest. Thus, *stasis*, often translated into English as 'corruption', undermines the ideal that citizens, unconcerned with the material consequences of their speech, will be free to think openly about what is in their city-state's best interests.

If the Athenians regarded politics as war conducted by other means, Popper regarded science as politics conducted by still other means. However, 'war', and by implication 'politics' and 'science', must be understood in a rather specific sense. Francis Fukuyama has usefully distinguished two ways of thinking about war – as a *struggle for survival* or a *struggle for recognition*. In these Darwinised days, we tend to presume that war arises from too many people chasing too few material resources: a struggle for survival. For example, at the writing of this book, a 'deep' explanation often given for US hostilities toward Iraq is the American need for access to Iraqi oil reserves. However, the Greeks envisaged warfare as arising under conditions of material abundance, not scarcity. A second-order, specifically cognitive scarcity was involved in the Greek struggle for recognition. Combatants struggle over who will be remembered by future generations. Nothing more clearly signals victory than that the histories told of the conquered are populated by descendants of the conquerors. Proof that we currently live in such a state of *second-order colonialism* is that 'our' history of science turns out to be a tale of great white males with unique mental powers – that is, people who look like heroic versions of today's professional scientists, our cognitive conquerors.

Imagine our bodies possessed by alien spirits whose hold over us is marked by the resistance they provide to what we might otherwise say or do. This is how second-order colonialism feels. (We shall become re-acquainted with this feeling below as the Cartesian 'evil demon'.) For example, today an aspiring biologist inclined toward divine creation is forced to deal with the theory of evolution by natural selection in one of two ways: either keep her own counsel and accept mental colonisation or publicly wage an uphill battle against evolution. The starkness of the choice shows that evolution is winning the struggle for recognition: it is presumed true, until proven otherwise. A Popperian science policy would enable the aspiring biologist to take this decision without inhibiting her capacity to take similar decisions in the future – especially if she turns out to be wrong. In other words, the ideas at stake would be sufficiently detached from the decider's personal circumstances that neither secular power nor financial advantage is bound to them. Only then can the ideas be considered solely on their merits. The alternative is the scientific equivalent of *stasis*.

Like most other philosophers and scientists, Popper was a kind of 'rationalist'. However, unlike most of them, he realised that rationality requires specific social and material conditions that are by no means 'natural' to the human condition but must be explicitly constructed and actively maintained. If there is any sense of 'unconditional commitment' in Popper's world-view, it is to maintaining just these conditions of free inquiry, something quite distinct from a Kuhnian commitment to a specific scientific paradigm. In Athens, this distinction was marked by the willingness of citizens to undertake military service even if they disagreed with the ruling party. Loyalty in the battlefield gave citizens credibility at the ballot box, the proper context for removing feckless leaders. Popper also saw this distinction at work in Søren Kierkegaard, who is now mainly remembered as the intellectual inspiration for existentialism. Kierkegaard's 'leap of faith' to Christianity gave him the courage to challenge the doctrines of particular Christian churches. Thus, for Popper, a genuine commitment to the truth gives scientists the courage to challenge the truth of particular theories, including the ones associated with a scientific paradigm. Such a commitment is demonstrated by upholding standards of criticism whose fate is independent of the fates of particular theories tested by them.

However, the 20th century witnessed the steady erosion of this crucial Popperian distinction. Science policy has regressed from a struggle for recognition to a struggle for survival. As universities increasingly abandon, or attenuate, the institution of tenure, and researchers are forced to depend on external grants, scientists have become all too keenly aware that one bad decision can ruin the material basis of their entire career. Therefore, it has become imperative to get it right the first time, ideally to be just slightly ahead of the pack – and better to run with the pack than way ahead of it. To Popper and his students, this strategic mentality, characteristic of Kuhnian normal science, revealed science's captivity to its social and material conditions.

Kierkegaard helped Popper forge the link between the critical spirit of classical Athens and the Protestant Reformation by making decision-making central to his thought. Indeed, Popper is not unfairly treated as a scientific existentialist. Kierkegaard characterised Christianity as a 'hypo-thesis' that one voluntarily undertakes in the full knowledge that the consequences are solely one's own – not God's – responsibility. God does not bargain with his creatures. Thus, in the Old Testa-ment, God mocks Job, the pious Jew who demands an explanation for his streak of grave misfortune: after all, God had neither forced Job to believe in him nor promised Job prosperity in return for faith. Similarly, for Popper, when a scientific knowledge claim is falsified, the responsibility lies solely with the scientist who proposed it – and not nature's failure to act in some desired fashion. The appropriate response is to hypothesise and test anew, not to rationalise the situation by claiming that the old hypothesis was 'really' true but somehow the test fell victim to factors beyond the scientist's control. The scientist might be prone to such rationalisation because of her research programme's past successes, but it is ultimately she who must take responsibility for the fate of her hypothesis. If this appears too high a standard, then science is in *stasis*.

For Popper, science is indeed in *stasis* – a 'fallen' state, a closed society, much as the Roman Catholic Church was when Martin Luther launched what became the Protestant Reformation. This is the spirit in which we should understand Popper's most radical follower, Paul Feyerabend, who in the 1970s called for the devolution of state support for science to local authorities and supported the proliferation of such anti-establishment forms of inquiry as Creationism, Deep Ecology and New Age medicine. Feyerabend's attitude toward science was closer to a Protestant's than an atheist's toward Christianity. Unfortunately, in our blinkered times, to be against the scientific establishment is to be against science itself.

Chapter 11

DO WE BELIEVE BY EVIDENCE OR BY DECISION? A VERY SHORT HISTORY OF EPISTEMOLOGY

We do not stumble upon our experiences, nor do we let them flow over us like a stream. Rather, we have to be active: we have to 'make' our experiences. It is we who always formulate the questions to be put to nature; it is we who try again and again to put these questions so as to elicit a clear-cut 'yes' or 'no' (for nature does not give an answer unless pressed for it). And in the end, it is again we who give the answer; it is we ourselves who, after severe scrutiny, decide upon the answer.

Karl Popper, *The Logic of Scientific Discovery*

Exploring an alternative theory by techniques like [trying to see the world through the theory's eyes], *one is likely to find that one is already using it (as one suddenly notes that one is thinking in, not translating out of, a foreign language). At no point was one aware of having reached a decision, made a choice. That sort of change is, however, conversion, and the techniques which induce it may well be described as therapeutic, if only*

111

because, when they succeed, one learns one had
been sick before. No wonder the techniques are
resisted and the nature of the change disguised in
later reports.

Thomas Kuhn, 'Reflections on My Critics'

Contemporary theories of knowledge rarely make reference to their religious roots. Nevertheless, these roots are indelibly marked in the philosophical tendency to think of beliefs as *compelled by evidence* rather than *made by decision*. Some philosophers even claim that it is psychologically impossible to decide to believe something. At best, such a decision is a pretence to belief (that is, to act 'as if' something were true); at worst, it is tantamount to wishful thinking. Clearly 'belief' is meant to be a rather profound state of mind, a partial revelation of the truth, no mere hypothesis adopted out of expedience or for the sake of argument. The problem of knowledge then revolves around the search for some foolproof method, or criterion, for assessing the evidential quality of beliefs.

Suspicion toward the role of decisions in belief formation goes back to the distinctive Christian state of *heresy*, which derives from the Greek for 'decision', specifically where one chooses to affirm something contrary to what one knows to be the case through acquaintance with church doctrine. A dialectic of dogma and heresy has thus characterised the history of Christianity. A major step in the secularisation of this dialectic came with the shift in the anchor point for 'probability' in the 17th century from established collective authority (dogma) to risky individual belief (heresy). Thus, the 'improbable' metamorphosed from doctrinal deviance to indefensible assertion. Both Kuhn and Popper drew on this history. Kuhn originally presented the inherent resistance of scientific paradigms to fundamental criticism under the rubric of 'dogma', and Popper frequently cast criticism in science as a risky personal choice made against the prevailing tide of collective opinion.

In defence of the view that evidence compels belief, epistemologists still cite the 1,500-year-old precedent of Saint Augustine (354–430), Catholic Bishop of Hippo, who refuted the Greek sceptics by claiming that some beliefs are self-evidently true because one would not have such beliefs unless their putative objects had caused them. Self-evident beliefs compel assent regardless of the other beliefs one holds. Thus, episodes of religious conversion and scientific discovery typically involve manifestations that upset one's expectations and intentions. However, since conversions and discoveries are normally portrayed as positive moments in cognitive development, it is easy to suppose that one's prior unreceptiveness consisted entirely of irrational prejudice. But this would be profoundly mis-leading. In fact, rational argument may be itself a major source of belief inhibition.

This point is important for appreciating the deep sense in which belief 'by evidence' and 'by decision' are opposed. Where rational argument is the sole standard for belief evaluation, most beliefs will fall short of the standard of deductive proof. In that case, a decision must be made, the consequences of which the decider then takes responsibility for. This was Popper's view. Kuhn, in contrast, adhered to the Augustinian maxim, often quoted by Wittgenstein, *crede ut intellegas* ('believe in order to understand'). In other words, we are sometimes forced to believe things on the basis of evidence without which we would not be inclined to believe – perhaps because we would otherwise have no reason to believe. Here one imagines St Paul's conversion to Christianity after having been thrown from his horse on the road to Damascus.

In his notorious 1975 book, *Against Method*, Paul Feyerabend depicted Galileo's status as the St Paul of Copernicanism in just this light. Contrary to the popular image of Galileo as someone who cham-pioned beliefs based on rational argument against a prejudiced Catholic establishment, Feyerabend

114

showed how Galileo had to resort to rhetoric to enhance 'evidence' supplied by an instrument that had been previously regarded as a toy (i.e. the telescope) in his efforts to overturn a wide range of reasoned objections. Had Galileo not already been a convert to Copernicanism, it is unlikely he would have had the determination – let alone the reason – to engage in these manoeuvres. By Popper's high ethical standards, Feyerabend's Galileo was a coward who tried to evade responsibility for his beliefs by hiding behind some dodgy data. But from Kuhn's more *Realpolitik* perspective, Galileo's irresponsible conviction paid off, as his various dialogues and debates provided clues that enabled others, especially Isaac Newton, to lay the foundations for a new physics.

Significantly, the modern founder of the quest for a foolproof method, the French philosopher René Descartes (1596–1650), had cast the problem of knowledge in terms of our ability to tell whether God or some evil demon had planted the evidence that compels our belief. What philosophers of science today call 'methodology' turns out to be a secularised version of the project of troubleshooting the sources of error in belief formation, until we are left with only one plausible explanation. Implicit here is that it would be presumptuous to think that we can ascertain the nature of reality by relying solely on our own cognitive resources. Rather, we must endeavour to discover whether God – or the evil demon – has called us to believe. Philosophers of science have called the object of this quest, the 'logic of discovery'. Once achieved, we shall know how to acquire the right frame of mind for receiving the revealed Word.

Not surprisingly, many of the landmark contributions to modern methodology have been made by theologians keen on demonstrating that only a divine hand could have crafted the order evidenced in nature. Prominent names in this vein include Christian Wolff, Thomas Bayes, William Paley and William Whewell – all scientist-theologians who flourished from the early 18th to the early 19th centuries. In the last 200 years, this tradition has been secularised as a search for 'transcendental justification' and 'inference to the best explanation'. Immanuel Kant and Charles Sanders Peirce are the most illustrious names associated with this development. It amounts to a subtle strategy of self-persuasion whereby we come to believe that the world could not appear as it does, were our beliefs fundamentally misbegotten. The ultimate explanation thus dispels all doubts. Our sheer inability to imagine an alternative, less edifying explanation for our deeply held beliefs is thus made into grounds for what the Jesuits call the 'moral certainty' of those beliefs. Of course, alternatively, our poor imagination may be the result of our having forgotten the circumstances under which we undertook our convictions in the first place. Such erasure of the contingency of the origins of our beliefs – especially the decisions that had to be made before the beliefs could be ours – is the stuff of Kuhn's Orwellian historiography of science, the seamier side of the search for the logic of discovery.

It is easy to see why Popper would have problems with this entire way of thinking about science. It basically reduces the search for knowledge to an exercise in fixing belief, and science itself to a 'quest for certainty', an expression that the American pragmatist John Dewey coined to capture what he saw as objectionable authoritarian strains in modern theories of knowledge – a hold-over from the days of state-established churches. Whereas Popper treated the scientific laboratory as a site for making decisions, each of which may be reversed by a later one, Kuhn regarded the laboratory as a site for engaging in practices that deepen the scientist's susceptibility to forming certain beliefs that will contribute to a clearer grasp of the vision of reality projected by her paradigm. Here Kuhn follows a long line of post-Augustinian thinkers from Blaise Pascal to the John Henry Newman for whom 'justified belief' or 'real assent' was characterised in most un-Popperian terms by a willingness to risk one's life on an idea through practical devotion, a return to the etymological roots of 'religion' in the enchanted ritualisation of life.

In the past 150 years, the secularisation of the logic of discovery has been marked by an increasing focus on the machine virtues of mathematical logic and computer algorithms. The result has been to dash any hope of realising Augustine's and Descartes' dream of a way to generate self-evidently true beliefs. To be sure, there are methods for generating (relatively) novel theories and for determining which of these are (relatively) true – but not both at once. All of this is music to Popperian ears because it means that people must always decide on which theories to pursue and take responsibility for their consequences. There are no epistemically respectable grounds for offloading responsibility on some phantom notion of 'evidence' (i.e. what I saw, you said, or the machine computed) as a shield against unpleasant outcomes. God would never open the door to such craven behaviour by forcing us to give up our intellectual independence in return for conformity to a method, paradigm, or conceptual framework that ensures the validity of our beliefs.

Of course, from Kuhn's standpoint, the situation

is rather different. For him, a scientist is not a fully self-realised human being, *à la* Popper, but a highly specialised version of *Homo sapiens*. Without the epistemic guarantees of a paradigm, it becomes difficult to motivate Kuhnian normal science. Nobody would reasonably undertake such a discipline unless she thought it would lead to the truth. However, Kuhn evaded this problem by availing himself of an approach to cognition provided by Jerome Bruner (b. 1915), an expert on psychological warfare during World War II who returned to Harvard to found its Center for Cognitive Studies. Today, Bruner is remembered for having extended his intellectual influences – the Gestalt psychologists, especially Egon Brunswik and Jean Piaget – into educational practice. However, his experimental research, epitomised in his 1956 book, *A Study of Thinking*, attracted much private and public funding in the Cold War for the way it defined 'conceptualisation'. Bruner operationalised this basic mental process as a quick and largely subliminal response to ambiguous stimuli in the environment.

In an amazing piece of Orwellian Newspeak, Bruner called these responses 'decisions', even though experimental subjects did not control the situations in which their response was demanded. Thus, Bruner's ideal subject would automatically produce the experimentally defined 'correct' response. The models for this sense of 'decision' came from modern warfare – determining the identity of an unexpected radar signal or a soldier advancing in the smoke-filled haze of the battlefield: friend or foe? Failure to act quickly and accurately could prove fatal. It is clearly a world in which the struggle for recognition has been reduced to a struggle for survival. The ideal soldier is not a clever deployer of discretion but a machine programmed to respond 'without thinking'. That Bruner should be taken to have demonstrated what is now called the 'theory-laden character of perception', as opposed to have reduced the process of theorising to sheer perception (a.k.a. 'pattern recognition'), is a mystery in the history of contemporary psychology.

Nevertheless, Bruner's influence on Kuhn and Kuhnians has been immense. The deliberative character of human thought, traditionally marked by hesitation prior to response and flexibility in the face of consequences, has been replaced by a perspective more closely aligned to an animal's adaptation to its ecological niche, where getting it right the first time and just in time is the ultimate sign of cognitive success. In Kuhn's case, the niche in question is neither the wild nor the battlefield but the scientific laboratory. Bruner's lesson to

Kuhn was that if design in nature is unlikely to be revealed in the normal course of inquiry, it can always be front-loaded through indoctrination into a preferred way of seeing things. Ironically, once the launch of the Soviet space satellite Sputnik in 1957 brought the Cold War to a fever pitch, Bruner (successfully) called for the dismantling of the Harvard general education programme in which *The Structure of Scientific Revolutions* was incubated. The reason, of course, was that the programme did not breed the sort of single-minded scientist that is especially needed in time of war.

CHAPTER 12

THE UNIVERSITY AS THE ABSENT PRESENCE OF THE KUHN–POPPER DEBATE

I would suggest that no successful institutionalisation of science (successful, that is, from the point of view of scientific progress alone) ever relied at all heavily on the judgment of a man's university's colleagues. I think that where science has flourished in the university setting, it has unfortunately been primarily by persuading the university, sometimes quite unwillingly, to relinquish its criteria of judgment in favor of those of the largely external professional community.

Thomas Kuhn, letter to Jerome Ravetz,
21 June 1972

The differences between Kuhn and Popper play into a far-reaching debate over the role of the university in society. However, the terms of this debate remain mostly implicit in their writings. For someone who regarded technical training as the most important social process in the maintenance and promotion of normal science, Kuhn said remarkably little about exactly where this training should occur, except that the venue should provide textbooks and laboratory equipment. Similarly, Popper, despite his own doctoral training in pedagogy, attended to the university's relevance to his scientific ideals only toward the end of his own academic career, largely in response to the threat to academic freedom posed by the military-industrial complex. Kuhn, who rose to international prominence during this period (the 1960s), remained studiously silent on the status of this challenge to his academic habitat, though it left a more indelible impression on the American than the British scene.

As the opening quote from Kuhn shows, the institutionalisation of scientific inquiry is far from obvious. Nevertheless, Kuhn and Popper could both agree that science requires an essentially social epistemology. The sustained pursuit of systematic knowledge means that certain social relationships must be maintained over time and space. But exactly which relationships? That depends on what sort of people we take scientists to be. How our protagonists entered the field of education makes a big difference here.

Popper began as a recruit to the reformist pedagogy of socialist Vienna, which saw the family as preventing children from realising their potential for critical and independent thought. But based on his own practical failures as a social worker,

Popper quickly came to believe that the emergence of an autonomous cognitive sensibility required much more than the mere removal of barriers to an inevitable process of development. Locally reinforced prejudices – theorised in the 1920s˙ as *Heimat* ('homeland') – provided children with a sense of order and legitimacy that the classroom could not easily replace. Moreover, Popper did not agree with the leading child psychology guru, the Neo-Freudian Alfred Adler, who held that children should be shown that socialist principles could provide the same sense of security as those of the family. For Popper, such 'demonstrations' amounted to indoctrination, since socialism – for all its intellectual attractions – had yet to empirically prove itself. Instead, Popper wanted children to learn to live with an unrelieved sense of insecurity as part of their development toward a genuinely critical perspective. In that case, children may decide to reject family values in favour of socialist ones, but only because they have agreed to assume responsibility for the outcome of a decision that neither history nor nature could guarantee.

Kuhn's pedagogical starting point and general orientation could not be more different. From the time he first taught science to non-scientists at Harvard to his later comparative studies of concept acquisition in scientists and children, Kuhn was effectively preoccupied with the problem of how science becomes someone's *Heimat*. How can an activity whose practice is so detached from everyday life and whose products so aspire to transcend their place of production nevertheless be the source of community for a band of devoted followers? Moreover, once he came to accept the premises of this question, Kuhn was then faced with the further problem of how such a tight-knit scientific *Heimat* manages occasionally to elicit striking innovations that end up 'revolutionising' the community of scientists.

To Popper and his followers, Kuhn's project reduced science education to an indoctrination strategy. In the 1920s, proto-fascist parties ridiculed Weimar Germany's tolerance for ambiguity and open-mindedness as disabling people from making any substantial commitments, thereby rendering them rootless. This return to roots was also echoed in the philosophical rhetoric of the day – most notably Martin Heidegger – as the search for a pre-linguistic 'Ground of Being' beneath the clatter of incommensurable discourses that littered public life. To Kuhn, Popper's relentlessly dialectical science was a formula for producing rootlessness, the remedy for which was to get at the 'tacit dimension' of science, whereby knowledge is most intimately tied to the scientist's 'being-in-the-world'.

From the Popperian standpoint, then, Kuhn's pedagogical heresy was to suggest that the scientific attitude, rather than being the great enemy of *Heimat*, in fact realised many of its qualities in an especially pure form. So is science about being rooted in the world, as Kuhn thought, or being uprooted, as Popper thought? A good way into this matter is by way of the most intriguing premise of Popper's theory of knowledge. Popper assumes that we possess *a priori false beliefs*, the revision and replacement of which provides the need for the systematic pursuit of inquiry, or science. In other words, humanity's special interest in knowledge arises not from some spontaneous sense of curiosity that beckons us to re-attach to the world, but from our having been born out of sorts with reality. It would not be far-fetched to think of this fallen state as the epistemic equivalent of 'Original Sin'. Moreover, like Original Sin, it is entirely possible to lead a passable secular life without ever fundamentally correcting those mental liabilities, and perhaps even being rewarded for them. Such is to live life as an animal. This is basically how Popper regarded normal scientists in their captivity to a Kuhnian paradigm.

Nowadays, psychologists have identified a range of 'hot' and 'cold' cognitive mechanisms that enable us to muddle through the human condition, whereby our liabilities simulate virtues under conditions that roughly correspond to everyday life. In other words, our prejudices and biases may function as 'heuristics' that expedite decision-making in a complex world. It is even sometimes claimed that these *a priori* false beliefs are 'evolutionarily adaptive', in that they are just good enough for the environments in which humans normally find themselves. However, as Popper would be the first to stress, science aspires to something greater than the path of least resistance to reality. The trick then is to come up with an arrangement of inherently fallible humans that enables them to produce a form of knowledge more substantial than they could produce left to their own devices.

In his epistemological sensibility, Popper follows in the footsteps of the philosophers of the 18th-century Enlightenment. Their common starting point may be summarised in the following principle: *The price of acquiring any knowledge at all is that it will be somehow distorted by the conditions of its acquisition; hence, criticism is the only universally reliable method.* Theology was the original Enlightenment target for this perspective, in which the findings of mechanics and the natural history of animals and humans functioned as critical instruments. In this context, the 'critical-historical method' was a thoroughly *moral* activity. Unlike previous Biblical scholars who had regarded, say, the Apostles' testimony of Christ's Resurrection as simply a statement of fact in which the Apostles' personal histories were of no relevance, the Enlightenment critics took seriously the Apostles' role in constructing the event as significant – and the long-term epistemic cost that heightened awareness may have incurred, even for those who take the general truth of Christianity as uncontroversial. The history of Biblical criticism, then, has been one long exercise in unpacking the universal dimension of Christ's message from its historical baggage.

By the time Popper followed Ernst Mach's lead, and generalised the critical-historical method as the scientific attitude, the process of unpacking the universal from the particular had been recast as the transformation of the *context of discovery* by the *context of justification*. Like the Bible, a historical account of a scientist's discovery is an alloy of blindness and insight whose 'rational reconstruction' must precede its evaluation as a knowledge claim. The two centuries that separated Popper's methodology from the theology of Spinoza and Pierre Bayle witnessed the migration of the critical-historical method from the free-thinking churches and salons to the university, where in the hands of

Wilhelm von Humboldt (1767–1835), famed first Rector of the University of Berlin, it became the touchstone for rediscovering that institution's original corporate autonomy.

Here it is worth recalling that until the 12th century, Roman law divided human interaction into two basic categories. In exceptional cases, legal protection was granted to limited social engagements (*socius*), such as business ventures and military expeditions, the point of which was to achieve goals set out by the people involved in them. Mission accomplished, the partners reverted to their default category of existence as members of particular families (*gens*), which were the means by which status and wealth were reproduced across generations. What had been lacking was a third category that would enable both individuals to acquire social identities other than the ones they inherited and collectives to pursue goals that transcend the interests of their current members. This third category came to be known in Roman law as *universitas*, which is best rendered as 'corporation', but contained universities among its earliest exemplars – along with craft guilds, churches, religious orders and city-states.

The revolutionary feature of the *universitas* was the legal recognition it gave to activities inherently worth pursuing by granting their practitioners a perpetual right to decide what counts as its worthy pursuit and who is worthy to pursue it. At last, humanity's sociology decisively broke with its biology, since the individuals delegated with transmitting the corporate activity over time were not necessarily, or even usually, members of the same family. This innovation was luminous in the context of Christendom, which attached great significance to the liberation of the human spirit from its material captivity. Thus, legally protected lineages based on common mental training rather than common physical ancestors became the *via regia* of institutionalised spirituality, which in secular garb (as 'credentials') has come to be the principal means by which social status is now recognised.

This point is obvious when made, but overlooked or misinterpreted when not. For example, the fact that the great contributors to modern physics – Newton, Faraday, Maxwell, Planck, Einstein – came from rather different social backgrounds is often mistaken to imply that scientific inquiry transcends society as such. On the contrary, it means that specific institutions have been constructed – notably universities – that are given licence to disrupt default patterns of societal reproduction on a regular basis in order to advance the fortunes of collective inquiry.

However, from its inception, the university has been divided over its sense of purpose. Today we might ask: Does the undergraduate or the graduate curriculum drive the university? Should the institution be oriented mainly to liberal or professional education? The Middle Ages expressed these two options in the ongoing struggle between Masters and Doctors, symbolised by the critical spirit of William of Ockham and the dogmatic spirit of Thomas Aquinas. Both sides of the dispute upheld what Humboldt was to immortalise in the early 19th century as the 'unity of teaching and research', but interpreted the charge in rather different ways. In our own time, Popper and Kuhn have re-invented the position of the Masters and the Doctors, respectively.

For the Masters, research is a by-product of teaching, specifically a Socratic reflection on the resistance that students pose to instruction. The object of research then becomes the liberation of 'spirit' (i.e. independent thinking) from 'matter' (i.e. untutored prejudice). The humanistic concern for disciplining the self through techniques of deep reading, critical thinking and effective speaking falls into this category. In contrast, for the Doctors, teaching is the vehicle for consolidating and distributing the latest research as an instrument of societal governance and an expression of personal expertise. Instead of removing the obstacles to full spirituality, here education gives the spirit focus and direction, a place in an institutional structure. The difference in academic attitudes evidenced by the Masters and the Doctors is perhaps best captured by Isaiah Berlin's classic distinction between 'negative' and 'positive' liberty, understood here as alternative goals for education.

Notwithstanding Humboldt's efforts, however, the universities never quite regained their original corporate autonomy in the 19th century, especially once they started to be harnessed with the task of reproducing successive generations of élites for the nation-state. In many respects, this transformation – ironically still associated with Humboldt's name – updated the Doctors' vision. The university's centrality to nation-building was accompanied by the growth of graduate instruction in traditional liberal arts subjects. Thus, for the first time, academic disciplines were formally conceptualised as jurisdictions with 'domains' and 'boundaries', on the model of the civil and ecclesiastical regions that had been administered by holders of medieval doctorates. These domains were surveyed in textbooks that increasingly combined the qualities of a training manual and a summary of established findings, which together equipped the novice with precedents for future practice, or colonisation of the uncharted domain. This rather late 19th-century conception of the textbook, tied to the consolidation of French and German national university systems locked in imperial struggle, is the preferred Kuhnian medium for the transmission of paradigm-based knowledge. Like other features of the model of scientific change presented in *The Structure of Scientific Revolutions*, this unique development is then generalised over the entire history of science.

So, what then happened to Humboldt's original ideal of 'unity of teaching and research'? Humboldt's vision was first expressed in an essay, *Ideas toward a Definition of the Limitations on State Action*, composed when he was only 25, nearly two decades before the peak of his influence in the Prussian Ministry of Education. This striking work portrayed the university as the place where people would acquire the skills they need for self-empowerment, which would then enable them to participate as active citizens in democratic assemblies. In the long term, the state would 'wither away' from its current overbearing paternalism to a purely administrative organ dedicated to implementing the considered judgements of the populace.

Humboldt's ideal of the university as weaning citizens off their dependency on state power, itself seen as a Hobbesian Leviathan that thrives on mass ignorance and fear, influenced many thinkers in subtle and profound ways. Marxists, of course, replaced the university with the party as the vehicle of state dissolution, though retaining much of that institution's original educational function – only now reformulated as indoctrination and propaganda. But Popper first felt the power of Humboldt's vision by looking behind John Stuart Mill's dedication of *On Liberty* to Humboldt, whose essay had been translated into English only a few years earlier – that is, 60 years after its original composition and long after the German universities had become engaged in nation-building.

It was through the Humboldt–Mill route that the spirit of the medieval Masters travelled, one that Popper (and the logical positivists) followed. Thus, they were ill-disposed to features of universities that rendered the institutions state-like, such as rigid disciplinary boundaries that treated scientific inquiry as if it were an abstract version of real estate development, as in the field today known as 'knowledge management'. However, knowledge as real estate arguably also applies to Kuhnian normal science. Certainly, the self-assigned task of post-Kuhnian philosophers of science has included underlabouring for the paradigms and disciplines that are taken to be the legitimate knowledge producers in their domains. Here it is worth recalling Larry Laudan's lament about the degradation of the Popperian demarcation problem in our time: Why do philosophers feel compelled to defend (and condemn) entire disciplines rather than evaluating individual knowledge claims on their own merits? Thus a Master queries the Doctors.

Unfortunately, the Doctors have been victorious, though the victory has turned out to be rather pyrrhic for the university's institutional integrity. The plot of this story is the aspect of Humboldt's legacy that Fritz Ringer has called *mandarinisation*, whereby German academics implicitly signed a Faustian pact with the state: the state would protect the universities, if the academics agreed to provide an ideological defence of the state or at least refrained from publicly criticising state actions. The bargain was rationalised with relative ease. Academics avoided politics by arguing that the ends of knowledge are either transcendentally presupposed by one's kind of inquiry or explicitly provided by the state. Both were politically safe options because neither invited critical reflection on the social conditions of one's own knowledge production. At the dawn of the 20th century, the distinction was epitomised in Germany by, respectively, the Neo-Kantian philosopher Heinrich

Rickert and the Neo-Hegelian economist Gustav Schmoller. It was in reaction to these two mandarins that Max Weber came to articulate the relationship between science and politics as vocations.

The mandarins treated their disciplines as guilds. In the Western legal tradition, the guild has been the corporate form most easily co-opted by a more powerful agent. Guilds officially enjoy an effective monopoly over the transmission of certain skills and products by virtue of their ability to maintain a consistently high level of quality. Historically, guilds acquired the conservative disposition of insurance bodies, censoring deviant practices that do not meet with the governing board's approval. In that sense, by enjoying a unique guild right of 'academic freedom', German academics became more politically manageable, since the state had no need to intervene to stop the spread of subversive positions, as the academics themselves would already find it in their collective interest to do so. Thus, the mutual criticism of the peer-review process simultaneously launders out more radical positions and insures that what remains is of sufficiently high quality to be appropriated for orthodox political purposes.

At the dawn of the 21st century, European science policy gurus have virtually reproduced the mandarin distinction between the transcendental and instrumental justification of inquiry in terms of what they call 'Mode 1' and 'Mode 2' knowledge production. Mode 1 stands for discipline-based research and Mode 2 for a hybridised sense of research that blends together the interests of academia, the state and industry. Seen stereoscopically, the origins of Mode 1 are pushed back to the founding of the Royal Society in the 17th century (if not the ancient Greek philosophers), while the roots of Mode 2 are brought up to the period starting with the Manhattan Project that built the first atomic bomb (if not the post-Cold War devolution of the welfare–warfare state). However, historically speaking, it is only in the last quarter of the 19th century – the Golden Age of mandarinisation – that *both* Modes come into being, almost simultaneously, in Germany. This corresponded to the mass assimilation of the laboratory-based natural sciences into the universities. Laboratories had been traditionally excluded from universities (and confined to polytechnics) for reasons that amounted to intellectualised class snobbery. Specifically, lab work required manual skills alien to the hands-free world of liberally educated élites for whom practical applications were an inferior form of knowledge. Yet, once the laboratory sciences were ensconced on campus, they quickly made alliances with state and industry clients, most notably in the Kaiser Wilhelm Institutes, the forerunners of today's Max Planck Institutes.

Two related features of mandarinisation are striking. First is the invisibility of the university as an institution that is more than the sum of its constituent departments. Second is the role of the natural sciences in anchoring knowledge production discourse – both in the original German and the contemporary European contexts. Weber struggled with the fact that the hyper-specialised sense of scientific inquiry associated with mandarinisation gained momentum with the academic rise of the natural sciences. For their part, the humanities were never as narrowly insular as Mode 1 implies but nor were they as readily adaptive to external pressures as Mode 2 implies. In that respect, the humanities has remained the bulwark of the university as an institution that is oriented toward knowledge without being exclusively beholden to either its resident specialists or its external clients. This is symbolised in that traditional nerve centre of university life, the undergraduate curriculum committee, where the relevance of each discipline's major discoveries to a liberal education needs to be negotiated on a regular basis.

Indeed, what had made the natural sciences so alien to the classical constitution of the university *also* enabled them, once inside the university, to adapt well to externally oriented research projects. Here it is worth recalling a salient feature of Kuhn's account of science, which is based entirely on the natural sciences: the 'normal science' conducted by a paradigm's practitioners is autonomous not only from practical applications but also from the research trajectories of other academic disciplines. In that respect, a paradigm is a *doubly alienated* form of knowledge – a self-contained module of inquiry that does not require the institutional setting of the university for its existence or even its legitimation. Although science policy gurus and knowledge managers make much of the increasing tendency of natural science faculties, especially in the biomedical sciences, to migrate off campus and metamorphose into training centres and research parks, this behaviour is merely a return to historic form for disciplines for whom the university was never their natural home.

Kuhn struggled with this ambivalent, if not largely negative, historic relationship between the natural sciences and universities. For him a major benchmark for scientific institutionalisation was the establishment of scientific academies in the Renaissance and the Enlightenment, especially the

Royal Society of London. However, these academies often justified their existence by pursuing scientific inquiry in ways that were specifically excluded by the universities. Moreover, unlike the sociologist Joseph Ben-David, Kuhn did not see a smooth institutional transition from the academies to the national universities in the modern period. Indeed, in Kuhn's own student days, President Conant had to introduce special professorships and bursaries to immunise Harvard's best researchers from the interdisciplinary charms of customised research facilities, funded by the philanthropic wing of big business.

In correspondence with Jerome Ravetz, quoted at the start of this chapter, Kuhn observes that the institutionalisation of paradigms as university departments has often required the intervention of education ministries, commercial interests and professional bodies that somehow managed to exert leverage over the local academics. But beyond advising Ravetz to read some articles by a recent Princeton Ph.D., Kuhn offers no further insight into the role of universities. Interestingly, that former Princeton doctoral student, R. Steven Turner, returned to the topic fifteen years later, arguing the flip-side of the issue – that without a formal academic base, a paradigm that cuts against the grain of established disciplines will have its influence dissipated in the long term, as members of the paradigm's network, lacking a mechanism for reproducing their collective work, regress to the norms of their home disciplines.

Turner's finding is worth recalling in an era when universities are increasingly fixated on 'knowledge management' strategies that identify dynamism with flexible networks rather than autonomous institutions. Too bad Kuhn himself never made the point. On the contrary, in correspondence with his brilliant student Paul Forman at the height of the Berkeley student revolts in 1964–5, Kuhn urged Forman to ignore thorny issues of university governance embroiling the campus and simply finish his dissertation. At one level, this is familiar advice, but it is also emblematic of someone who could never quite call the university home.

CHAPTER 13

POPPER AND ADORNO UNITED: THE RATIONALIST LEFT AT POSITIVISM'S WAKE

The original function of the Left was to be for the underdogs, and that was very good. But then this function became perverted.

Karl Popper, 'Once More Against
Historicism' (1991 interview)

Popper was always swimming against the intellectual current of his times in two senses. First, he was a resolutely dialectical thinker who developed his positions against the dominant discourses of the day. Thus, most of Popper's supposedly positive views were really negative ones in disguise: his deductivism was anti-inductivism, his liberalism anti-authoritarianism, his individualism anti-holism. Consequently, Popper often presented his views as critical sketches that presuppose acquaintance with the details and history of what is being criticised. Second, the 20th century has accelerated the 'outsourcing' of philosophical problems, if not to the special sciences themselves, at least to philosophical sub-disciplines (or sub-philosophical disciplines?) that shadow those sciences. Thus, Popper's readers who are interested in, say, his falsificationist methodology, his political liberalism, his philosophy of social science and his evolutionary epistemology tend to fall into four distinct camps – none with an interest in trying to put all the pieces together.

Popper was, of course, not alone in having left a fragmented philosophical legacy. So too did another exiled German-speaking Jew of Popper's generation who tried to construct a general worldview from outside the philosophy establishment. I refer here to Popper's other sparring partner in the 1960s, Theodor Adorno (1903–69). Adorno, like Popper, was a dialectical thinker who denied the idea of 'philosophy degree zero'. But where Popper opposed the so-called neutral observation language of the logical positivists, Adorno contested the supposedly positionless 'jargon of authenticity' advanced by existential phenomenologists like Martin Heidegger (about whom more in chapters 15–16). Nevertheless, Adorno's fate has resembled Popper's in an important respect: his high modernist aesthetics, Hegelian epistemology, Marxist sociology and post-Holocaust ethics have attracted four discrete audiences. Indeed, today Adorno is typically known second-hand. He is recognised as the intellectual leader of the first generation of the 'Frankfurt School', a species of critical social theory that is nowadays most closely associated with Adorno's student, Jürgen Habermas, who has done much to shift the School's philosophical centre of gravity from German Marxism to American pragmatism.

The Frankfurt School began as the Institute for Social Research in Frankfurt, a typical product of the Weimar Republic, Germany's culturally rich and politically volatile inter-war regime that gave the country its first taste of constitutional democracy. The Institute was one of several think-tanks established by enlightened capitalists in the 1920s to assuage their guilty consciences. Specifically, in the wake of the dubious precedent set by the 1917 Bolshevik Revolution in Russia, the 'Frankfurt School' was funded to enable a politically gradualist transition from capitalism to socialism. Specifically, it engaged in a propaganda campaign to get people to adopt a world-view that would lead them to no longer desire, or at least regard more ambivalently, the commodities produced by the increasingly capitalised 'culture industries', which included the mass media and their incursion into more traditional art forms. Such indefinitely long-term mental preparation was seen as necessary before any specific political activity could be sanctioned.

Here we see an important difference in the early political sensibilities of Adorno and Popper. In contrast with Adorno, Popper flirted with several explicitly politicised courses of action, including the organisation of consumer collectives and the promotion of critical pedagogy in schools. To be sure, Popper was rather easily put off by the hurly-burly of democratic politics, but retained his suspicion of historicist-inspired political com-placency. Nevertheless, after years of exile in the UK and the US respectively, Popper and Adorno returned to Germany in 1961 to launch what, over the rest of that decade, came to be known as the *Positivismusstreit* – literally the 'conflict over positivism' – in German social theory. The debate was supposedly about the methodology appro-priate for social science research. But Popper and Adorno talked more about general epistemological attitudes than protocols for sociological inquiry. And though pitted as antagonists, they resembled each other much more than either resembled, respectively, the analytic philosophers of science and the cultural studies practitioners with whom they are normally associated today. Such is the extent to which the unregulated division of labour in the sciences has undermined the quest for a holistic philosophical vision.

Moreover, in the specific case of Popper and

Adorno, the changing political fortunes of Marxism have added to the confusion. The result has been to divide the forces of what I call the *rationalist left*, thereby opening the door to the rightward, so-called neo-liberal, anti-rationalist drift that has characterised the 'postmodern condition'. The rationalist left consists of the combined forces of critique that in the 1960s came to be officially divided into 'critical theory' (Adorno and his Marxist followers) and 'critical rationalism' (Popper and his more liberal followers). In the long term, the *Positivismusstreit* not only dissipated the forces of critique in the academy but also subverted any united defence of the university as a site of auto-nomous inquiry.

All started well. After the original Popper–Adorno exchange at the 1961 meeting of the German Sociological Association in Tübingen, the rapporteur, the sociologist Ralf Dahrendorf, observed that there was remarkably broad agree-ment between the two men, marking *both* as staunch anti-positivists. Adorno and Popper targeted the same foes, notably the style of 'grand theorising' and 'abstracted empiricism' spawned by structural-functionalist sociology, which two years earlier had been lampooned by C. Wright Mills for betraying 'the sociological imagination'. Moreover, Popper and Adorno were even agreed on the tendency of experimental psychology and theo-retical economics to obscure, if not outright deny, the background social conditions that ultimately determine the validity of their generalisations. This made both sworn enemies of what Popper called 'essentialism' in social science, opposing *both* any psychologism or economism that would reduce society to the sum of atomic individuals *and* any social holism that would reduce the individual to the sum of her social roles. Rather, Popper and Adorno followed Max Weber in regarding the social world as a field defined by countervailing tendencies in terms of which the potential of individuals is realised.

Adorno and Popper equally disowned the idea of disunified science and its implied underlabouring approach to philosophy that is popular not only in our Neo-Kuhnian world but also in the Neo-Kantian academic environment in which both were trained. For them, disciplinary boundaries are not epistemically significant. On the contrary, they inhibit the capacity for independent critical judgement on the current state of knowledge and impede the drive toward a unified understanding of reality. Moreover, neither Adorno nor Popper believed that the categories of the natural sciences are inherently closer to reality than those of the social sciences. The categories of both sets of fields involve socio-historically conditioned choices, the ultimate value of which rests on their consequences. For both, this sense of contingency in the development of knowledge, which hints at alternative trajectories, fuelled the critical imagination.

Overall, then, Popper and Adorno shared an Enlightenment vision of the social role of philosophy: philosophy questions the taken-for-granted beliefs of common sense. They strenuously opposed any rearguard 'language therapy' approach that would have philosophy itself interrogated by common sense (Wittgenstein) or, worse, by some primordial pre-philosophical sensibility (Heidegger). In addition, they denied any sharp division of labour between philosophy and sociology, say, along Vilfredo Pareto's influential strategy of assigning to philosophy the task of explaining the 'rational' and to sociology the 'irrational' forces in society. Rather, Popper and Adorno treated the relationship between the two disciplines in more complementary terms, say, as akin to mind and body or form and matter.

Significantly, Adorno and Popper differed on the current state of the Enlightenment project. Whereas Adorno held that both totalitarian fascism and consumer capitalism have taken the Enlightenment to its self-destructive extreme, Popper held that the Enlightenment has yet to be fully realised. Corresponding to this difference in perspective was the implication that each drew from the Weberian dictum that science is 'value free'. For Adorno it meant that science was an instrument of pure power, whereas for Popper it meant that science had developed binding means for deciding between theories.

What probably made the amount of agreement between Adorno and Popper seem so surprising – especially to younger listeners (Dahrendorf himself was only 32 in 1961) – was the vivid opposition between Marxism and liberalism that characterised the Cold War political landscape. Here it is worth recalling the free intercourse between Marxism and liberalism that transpired under the fluid rubric of 'social democracy' in the Weimar Republic, the formative period for both Popper and Adorno. 'Social democracy' in this sense was opposed to any political position – from conservative religious groups to more reactionary monarchist and fascist parties – that upheld the need for a higher authority than the rule of law. In this respect, Popper's steadfast opposition to authoritarianism remains well-known, but it is sometimes forgotten that Adorno co-authored the landmark empirical psychological study, *The Authoritarian Personality* (1950) during his exile in the United States.

The dismemberment of the social democratic imagination can be charted by the increasing puzzlement and criticism that this book attracted, as the Cold War progressed. In particular, as Stalin replaced Hitler as the enemy of American liberalism, challenges were made to Adorno's identification of 'egalitarianism' as an anti-authoritarian trait. Thus, by 1954 the sociologist Edward Shils had coined the phrase 'left-authoritarian' and began the tendency to dismiss *The Authoritarian Personality* as methodologically flawed by its now-demonised 'leftist' political agenda. Popper's followers tended to gravitate to Shils' position. Nevertheless, what most readily marked Popper and Adorno as old Weimar leftists was their (admittedly rather different) attempts to fashion a critique of capitalist society from the *consumption*, rather than the production, side of the Marxist equation.

Both Popper and Adorno realised that Marx's wishful prediction that the proletarian revolution would be launched in the nation with the best-organised labour movement in the late 19th century, Germany, was not only false but also unlikely ever to take place. The question then was how to design an effective resistance to capitalism's resilient nature. Both found critique to be an attractive *modus operandi* because they realised that people would need to come to regard the products of capitalism differently before any substantial change was possible. Nevertheless, for Popper, the Frankfurt School's propaganda campaign betrayed the worst features of historicism. Adorno presumed that he already knew not merely *that* something was wrong with capitalism, but exactly *what* was wrong with it. Thus, Adorno set himself the task of converting consumers to his own incorrigible beliefs, rather than testing his fallible knowledge claims against consumer response. Ironically, Adorno's superior epistemic attitude only led him to an increasingly timid political stance. The 40-year failure of the Frankfurt propaganda campaign pointed to capitalism's unanticipated strength, which in turn spurred Adorno to propagate an intensified – and arguably increasingly obscurantist – version of the original critique.

In practice, this meant that Adorno and his colleagues left the political arena open to others, typically less enlightened folk who, unburdened by a sense of epistemic superiority, have been happy to try their luck in the ballot box and the market-place. Beneficiaries have included Adolf Hitler and J. Walter Thompson. (The juxtaposition of the Nazi dictator and the Madison Avenue giant is deliber-ate, given the role of the Weimar media mogul Alfred Hugenberg in managing Hitler's rise to power.) In contrast, by refusing to make their mistakes in public, the Frankfurt School ensured that the revolution would remain indefinitely deferred. However, this central weakness in the left's political rationality never fully surfaced in the *Positivismusstreit*. Instead, the point of rupture between Popper and Adorno turned more directly on differences over manner of expression.

CHAPTER 14

POPPER AND ADORNO DIVIDED: THE RATIONALIST LEFT HAUNTED BY HISTORICISM

Is it not possible, or even likely, that contemporary scientists know less of what there is to know about their world than the scientists of the 18th century knew of theirs? Scientific theories, it must be remembered, attach to nature only here and there. Are the interstices between those points of attachment perhaps now larger and more numerous than ever before?

Thomas Kuhn, 'Logic of Discovery or Psychology of Research?'

The opaqueness of astrology is nothing but the opaqueness prevailing between various scientific areas that cannot be meaningfully brought together. Thus one might say that irrationality is in itself the outgrowth of the principle of rationalizations that was evolved for the sake of higher efficiency, the division of labor. What Spengler calls 'the modern caveman' dwells in the cavity, as

*it were, between organized sciences that do not
cover the universality of existence.*

Theodor Adorno, 'The Stars Down to Earth'

Popper and Adorno shared the critic's tendency to
presuppose that the audience already knows the
target of criticism in some detail, so that one's own
discourse becomes a series of reflections on the
hidden opponent. This feature made it frustrating
for listeners who sought constructive advice on the
conduct of social research. But more importantly,
the two antagonists expressed their critiques in
radically different forms. Popper provided a list of
theses, with which he wanted Adorno to agree or
disagree. In response, Adorno, seeing very little
with which to disagree, decided instead to dwell on
the care with which one needs to formulate
epistemological claims in the human sciences so
that they are not captured by an unreflective and
potentially oppressive positivism. In other words,
Adorno criticised Popper for not being sufficiently
'reflexive' in considering how his words might be
used to legitimise projects to which he (and
Adorno) would be opposed.

Admittedly, Popper was more sanguine than
Adorno about the precedent set by the success of
the physical sciences. At the same time, Popper
operated with a rather sophisticated and somewhat

idealised understanding of scientific method that, for example, refuses to see empirical regularities as necessarily indicative of scientific laws, if they have not been first subjected to rigorous experimental tests that control for whatever biases, or 'anchoring effects', may be hidden in the initial conditions under which the phenomena are observed. Adorno understood this feature of Popper's view, but equally saw that it could be easily misunderstood as endorsing a mindlessly positivist conversion of regularities to laws. Thus, Adorno might ask Popper: 'If your view of physics as the vanguard of inquiry applies only under ideal experimental conditions – which hardly ever obtain in the social sciences – then what good is it as a normative standard?' In other words, Adorno criticised Popper for not being sufficiently 'reflexive' in considering how his words might be used to legitimise projects to which he (and Adorno) would be opposed.

Where Adorno and Popper genuinely differed was on the scope of the consequences and the means of assessment used for evaluating, say, scientific theories: does one proceed (*à la* Adorno) by demystifying the ideology that masks the power relations a theory sustains or (*à la* Popper) by designing experimental tests for the outcomes that the theory predicts? A sign of the alienated nature of critique in today's world is that these two approaches are seen as antagonistic and perhaps even mutually exclusive, from a logical point of view. This is especially unfortunate because, once again, surface differences serve only to conceal a deeper unity of purpose. As to be expected, this schism is the product of mutual misunderstanding.

The interpretive policy of ideology critique proposed by Adorno (and many other Marxists) is typically misread as claiming that the politically incorrect *origins* of a scientific theory somehow impugn the theory's validity. For logicians, this is to commit the *genetic fallacy*. However, the facts that truly concerned Adorno are, like Popper, the ones that *follow* from a theory's acceptance. Where Popper and Adorno truly differ is that Adorno treats scientific theories as systematic attempts to predict and control a world that contains *both* theorised objects and theorising subjects. In that respect, much more was always at stake in criticism for Adorno than for Popper. According to Adorno, a validated scientific theory simultaneously enables its possessor to exert power over a part of reality and the people interested in it. The main reason Popper modelled his version of criticism on the controlled laboratory experiment is that it precisely avoids this situation, whereby risking ideas starts to look like risking lives. Popper believed that to be both effective and humane (i.e. improvable in light of new evidence), criticism must operate at a narrower gauge than that of ideology critique. For Adorno, Popper's approach was too idealistic to function effectively as critique.

Nevertheless, this difference between Popper and Adorno is better seen as concerning specific tactics than general strategy. The strategy was also shared by another German-speaking émigré with whom both locked horns, namely, the sociology of knowledge's most influential thinker, Karl Mannheim (1893–1947). Mannheim defeated Adorno for the chair in sociology at the University of Frankfurt shortly before fleeing the Nazis, after which he reinvented himself, alongside Popper, at the London School of Economics. In a nutshell, Mannheim combined Adorno's totalising sense of critique with Popper's openness to political reform in his self-appointed task of 'reconstructing' society in an era of mass democracy. But whereas Popper might try to alter the false beliefs of the masses by challenging them on their face, Mannheim would develop policies for eliminating the background conditions that have made the views plausible. What Popper would resolve by debate in the open forum, Mannheim would pre-empt by educational reform and more global forms of social planning.

The point worth highlighting here is that Popper did not disagree with Mannheim's substantive knowledge claim that certain social conditions render certain beliefs more plausible than others and that these conditions have been and can be changed. Rather, Popper was disturbed by the institutional framework within which Mannheim's claim would become the basis for action. This framework struck Popper as authoritarian. Not only does it shield Mannheim's own knowledge claims from social-scientific scrutiny but more importantly it denies people the opportunity to decide for themselves whether they accept the validity of Mannheim's claims. In that sense, Mannheim dehumanises the people he is trying to save by disarming their capacity for rational judgement, in effect denying their right to be wrong. This is also the spirit in which Popper's notorious condemnation of psychoanalysis and Marxism as 'pseudo-sciences' should be taken.

Popper's suspicions about Adorno and Mannheim stemmed from what he regarded as their latent historicism, which in this context figures very much as gnosticism does in Christianity. Both historicism and gnosticism blaspheme by claiming a kind of access to the divine plan that is normally lacking in humans. This in turn causes historicists and gnostics to disregard ordinary political conventions. However, two radically different courses of action may follow from this sort of historicism, both of which were in evidence in the Weimar period.

The first, associated with the social democrats and other 'establishment Marxists', was complacency in the face of mounting support for right-wing movements, especially Nazism. According to Marxist theory, these movements were merely the last gasp of a dying capitalism that would prove incapable of launching a credible set of policies. Thus, there was no need to add to the credibility of these movements by publicly contesting their claims. The second course of action, associated with just those movements, was marked by a more aggressively expressed disregard for the public sphere, in the form of ruthless propaganda and terror campaigns. The passivity of the former and the activity of the latter conspired to enable Hitler to be democratically elected Chancellor of Germany in 1933.

To recall Max Weber's terminology, both the social democrats and the fascists were driven more by conviction than by responsibility. Both sides were convinced that the truth was theirs. But whereas the social democrats waited for the time of delivery, the fascists felt impelled to seize it. Both, in their different ways, cared little for the consequences of, respectively, inaction and action. While still involved in Viennese leftist politics as a young man, Popper had called for verbal and armed engagement with the fascists, decrying the relatively tolerant attitudes that had met their activities.

Popper appeared to be sensitive to what mass communications researchers nowadays call the 'spiral of silence', namely, the tendency in democratic societies for public opinion to drift toward a minority position that has repeated exposure and little formal opposition – perhaps because, as in the case of Hitler, none of the *bien pensant* intellectuals of the day thought he would ever be taken seriously. One explanation for this phenomenon, which Popper could appreciate, is that in democracies citizens presume that the channels of political communication are active media equally open to all, which makes it reasonable to assume that objections to a position will be publicly expressed and not simply assumed to be self-evident.

Popper's responses to Adorno and Mannheim re-enact the twin bogeys he originally identified with historicism. This ultimately explains Popper's alienation from his leftist comrades. On the one hand, Adorno was like the social democrat who, secure in the belief that he understands the course of history, waits in perpetuity for the right moment to come when esoteric critique can be effectively translated into emancipatory action. Such waiting (for Godot?) is supposedly justified because the power of critique could prematurely destabilise the social order. This patronising, even Platonic, attitude toward the public offended Popper's democratic instincts and was politically refuted by the spiral of silence. On the other hand, Mannheim, though certainly no fascist, reproduced a tamer version of the Leninist impulse to let his conviction in the truth of his views license an irreversible policy of social transformation to make the world conform to those views. In this case, the leftist is not so much patronising as contemptuous of a public who appears as little more than a mobilisable resource and potential source of (reactionary) resistance.

Nevertheless, in the final analysis, Popper, Adorno and Mannheim were united against a common foe, which unfortunately they tended to see in each other. That foe is the fatalistic turn of mind that Popper associated with historicism – *that things could not be other than they are*. This turn of mind appears in many guises, ranging from hyper-rational trust in science to irrational despair of science, which define the limits of what all three would have recognised as the 'pseudo-scientific'.

On the one hand, there is a sense of the inevitability of progress associated with 'scientific realism' that proposes, in Hilary Putnam's famous formulation, that the success of science would be a miracle, were it not getting closer to the truth. Here success is simply identified with self-reinforcing tendencies in the accumulation of capital, status and worldly power – as well as explanatory scope and predictive accuracy – associated with the dominant sciences of the day. The image corresponds to the Orwellian historiography that Kuhn associated with a paradigm's self-understanding. Thus, one does not consider, say, the opportunity costs of scientists having decided to pursue one research trajectory instead of another, or whether other research orientations, provided with similar resources and control over the criteria by which their work is judged, might not equally have demonstrated the same levels of 'success'. By suppressing such contingencies in the history of science, the hyper-rationalist downplays the responsibility of particular scientists (and their funders, users, etc.) for particular decisions that have shaped the course of inquiry. It is as if science were driven by Divine Providence, and only one decision must be made – to walk with the saints or the sinners.

On the other hand, there is the irrationalist impulse that both Popper and Adorno associated with the modern resurgence of astrology. This began in the Weimar Republic as a by-product of the general disillusionment with natural science after Germany's defeat in World War I. A war triggered by diplomatic mishap that was ultimately lost by the scientifically most advanced nation caused many to question humanity's control of its fate. Adorno caught a second wave of this sentiment during his stay in Los Angeles early in the Cold War, when many Americans turned to astrology to 'cope' with what was felt to be an inevitable nuclear showdown. At one level, the critical perspective shared by Popper and Adorno updates the original theological objection to astrology: astrology locates the causes of human behaviour in celestial phenomena so far removed from one's ordinary sphere of action that it discourages people not only from acting decisively but also from taking responsibility for whatever they do. However, the specifically modern cast of the Popper–Adorno objection to astrology is that it provides a spurious unity of understanding in a world of hyper-specialisation, something that Kuhn himself regarded as simply inevitable. Instead of trying to resolve the deep-seated tensions between disciplinary practices that currently impede any global understanding, astrology purports to transcend these interdisciplinary tensions – and the conflicting cognitive standards associated with them – by providing direct links between the origin of things in the heavens and our destinies on Earth.

It is worth noting that today astrology is hardly alone in cultivating this form of irrationalism. The demographic and climatological models used to forecast ecological crises often concentrate the policy imagination on, say, carbon emissions from the combustion of fossil fuels, while deferring more direct solutions to problems relating to poverty and development (which would involve political and economic regime changes, both in the developed and the developing worlds). Deep in their causal reach, remote in their projected consequences, and abstract in their formulation, these models often lower policy-makers' aspirations to the mere mitigation of effects from impending disaster from far-away sources. Something similar may be said about the attempts by self-styled 'socio-biologists', 'evolutionary psychologists' and 'behavioural geneticists' to trace complex features of the human condition directly to bits of DNA on the human genome, bypassing our knowledge of history and the social sciences. The result is to evacuate the sphere of practical politics by reducing the possibilities for action to a choice between 'play God' and 'accept fate'.

Not surprisingly, Adorno and Popper captured each other's weak points beautifully but failed to address their own. For the many social and natural scientists who found in Popper a source of legitimation, he was indeed regarded as Adorno feared, an accessible positivist who could be used to justify what Kuhn called 'normal science'. This was simply because Popper forcefully articulated the ideal to which many scientists aspired without being quite as forceful in criticising their failure to achieve the ideal in their practice. This discrepancy eventually opened the door to the new sociology of science, or science studies, whose scandalous reputation lies precisely in revealing the myriad ways in which scientists' words and deeds are at odds with each other. Unfortunately, most science studies practitioners respond to their discovery by suggesting that Popper-style normative discourse be junked altogether in favour of modes of legitimation that enable the scientists to carry on with their day-to-day business with the least resistance.

As for Adorno, his progeny in cultural studies have tended to fixate on his defence of 'difficult writing' as a form of reflexive resistance against hegemonic ideological structures that have the potential to co-opt the words of authoritative academics for their own purposes – as Adorno believed, perhaps rightly, had happened in Popper's case. However, in practice, Adorno's strategy has equally led to a dissipation of the critical impulse, as the criticised hegemons typically do not recognise themselves in the criticism – mainly because they cannot make sense of it. The result, of course, is that the so-called critiques launched by cultural studies have failed to hit their intended targets, who cannot see the point of a response. Indeed, the pointlessness of this form of pseudo-critical non-exchange was notoriously publicised in the parody known as the Sokal Hoax, whereby a disgruntled US physicist, Alan Sokal, managed to publish an article in a leading cultural studies journal that turned out to be a mix of impenetrable jargon, politically correct references and bogus accounts of technical physics.

The irony of Adorno's and Popper's fates is traceable to their failure to capitalise on their points of agreement. Both regarded philosophy and sociology as mutually reinforcing, not antagonistic, disciplines. In other words, one cannot adequately theorise about the aims and norms of inquiry without considering the institutional frameworks in which they might be realised. For this reason, both Adorno and Popper are worthy progenitors of my own project of social epistemology. Nevertheless, neither engaged sufficiently with the policy issues that emerge from this union of philosophy and sociology. Both were too suspicious of social institutions to ever endorse any specific embodiment of their ideals. By failing to associate their ultimate ends with any secular means – be it a church, a political party, or the university – Adorno and Popper effectively crossed the imaginary line from criticism to nihilism.

In the second round of the debate, Popper and Adorno were replaced by members of the younger generation – Hans Albert and Jürgen Habermas. In this context, Adorno's friendly criticism of Popper was magnified into a major ideological dispute. Habermas especially drove home the idea that Popper's 'straight-talking' approach was politically and intellectually naïve, especially during the increasing social unrest of the late 1960s. It was only after this explicit assertion of the *superiority* of the Frankfurt School's 'dialectical' critique that Popper's defenders began to demonise Adorno's followers as irrationalists and totalitarians. Soon thereafter came the dissolution of the rationalist left, a contemporary version of the Fall in whose aftermath progressive thinkers labour today.

Intellectual life has paid a heavy toll from the failure of the two great modern exponents of the rationalist left to offer a new legitimation for the university when it was needed in the 1960s. Consequently, we live in a polarised intellectual universe defined by, on the one hand, Habermas (the only person whose reputation truly benefited from the *Positivismusstreit*) and, on the other, Jean-François Lyotard's famous anti-university tract of the late 1970s, *The Postmodern Condition*. Thus, the university has been reduced to either a pure transcendental idea – or 'ideal speech situation' – unrelated to any actual institutional manifestation (Habermas) or a pure physical space in which various unrelated knowledge-based activities are transacted (Lyotard). The clearest sign of our 'post-academic condition' is the increasing tendency to sever matters of research from those of teaching, so that the production of new knowledge is increasingly placed in more élite hands (through intellectual property legislation), while the curriculum is narrowly focused on putative job skills. The idea of 'general education' as a crucible for the incorporation of new knowledge into a curriculum that would equip all students for critically facing the future is fading into the distant past. Kuhn might be relieved, but Popper would be furious.

· CHAPTER 15 ·

HOW TO BE RESPONSIBLE FOR IDEAS – THE POPPERIAN WAY

... my guess is that should individual scientists ever become 'objective and rational' in the sense of 'impartial and detached', then we should indeed find the revolutionary progress of science barred by an impenetrable obstacle.

Karl Popper, 'The Rationality of Scientific Revolutions'

Among those inspired by Popper's *The Open Society and Its Enemies* was the French political sociologist Raymond Aron (1905–83), whose 1955 book, *The Opium of the Intellectuals*, sparked the genre known as the 'critique of intellectuals'. However, there is a significant difference in context between Popper and Aron, on the one hand, and their recent American emulators, Richard Wolin, Mark Lilla and Tony Judt, on the other. Both groups of writers are preoccupied with, *inter alia*, Nazis and Communists. But Popper and Aron criticised intellectuals who supported Nazi Germany or the Soviet Union at times (the 1940s and 1950s respectively) when those regimes might have still turned out to be world-historic winners. Their critical standpoint was not dependent on the course of world history. This exposed them to political risk, had the totalitarians been victorious. In contrast, most critiques today target intellectuals and regimes that *at the time of writing* are uncontroversially regarded as world-historic losers. The Nazi and Soviet examples common to the two generations of critics make it easy to overlook the fact that nowadays critique is rarely, if ever, applied to intellectuals who have benefited, perhaps more passively, from regimes that have turned out to be world-historic *winners*. In this respect, the Nazi Martin Heidegger (1889–1976) is a much softer target for intellectual critique than, say, the Cold Warrior Thomas Kuhn.

Heidegger is such a pivotal figure for our analysis because knowledge of his Nazi past has corresponded with his elevation to the top echelon of 20th-century philosophers. To be sure, in one important respect, Heidegger stood on the same side as his contemporaries Wittgenstein, Carnap, Popper and Adorno: all were disillusioned by academic philosophy's failure to provide direction to the increasingly diverse forms of knowledge that abounded in the Weimar Republic. Instead, they found – as one finds today – philosophers simply performing underlabouring service for the special sciences. (Back then, the philosophers were 'Neo-Kantian'; today they are 'Neo-Kuhnian'.) However, Heidegger was distinguished by his deep roots in Catholic theology, which led him to associate philosophy's fallen status with a loss of spiritual rootedness in the world more generally – the solution to which required a turn back to basics, or 'Being-in-the-world'. Thus, Heidegger became the philosopher of the 'homeland', or *Heimat*, for which the Nazi Party became the principal political outlet. Heidegger courted the Nazis, and once in power, they appointed him Rector of Freiburg University, a post he held for a year before he realised that the Nazis were not closely following his advice. At that point he went into self-imposed exile without ever renouncing Party affiliation. The significance of Heidegger's silence was investigated by the De-Nazification commission after World War II, but all it got were evasive answers that left the matter unresolved. What is clear, however, is that for his remaining 30 years, Heidegger never declared a change of heart or mind about the Nazis or his involvement with them.

That the critical gaze should be nowadays so firmly fixed on intellectuals aligned with world-historic losers like Heidegger is somewhat surprising. The critics tend to be, like Aron, political realists who hold that there are no unmitigated goods or unsullied agents in the world: even the most ethical course of action will exact its own costs and casualties. This is sometimes called, after the existentialist philosopher Jean-Paul Sartre, the doctrine of *dirty hands*. The critique of intellectuals gets its bite from the Popperian point that it is sometimes possible to anticipate consequences that one does not intend: our hands could perhaps have been less dirty than they turned out to be. The social responsibility of intellectuals is tied to a heightened sense of circumspection about such counter-factual possibilities, which reflect our ability to learn from the past. Specifically, we must be scrupulous about tracking *both* the positive and the negative consequences of ideas that are advanced in the public domain.

There are two versions of the doctrine of dirty hands, both of which refer to negative unintended consequences. The relevant consequences may derive from either well-intentioned acts or simple failures to act. The former, associated with what natural law theorists call the *doctrine of double effect*, has been the subject of much discussion, especially in relation to the ethics of war. But in discussing Kuhn's status as 'Cold Warrior', we shall be concerned with the latter situation, which utilitarian moral philosophers have regarded as the basis for *negative responsibility*, that is, responsibility for what one does not do. Thus, if your having acted in a certain way would have increased the good of many and the suffering of few, then your failure to act is tantamount to your having acted badly. In this spirit, Sartre blamed the studiously apolitical but well-positioned Gustave Flaubert for the repression of the Paris Commune in 1871 because Flaubert did nothing to prevent it. Clearly, negative responsibility is a burden that especially falls on those with power and influence, since it is typically they who could have made a difference.

A price perhaps paid by world-historic victors is a moral coarseness that blinds them to the demands of negative responsibility, since failure to meet its demands corresponds to compliance with the vindicated regime. When the final outcome of the Cold War was in doubt, American intellectuals were very sensitive to the difference that their inaction might make to their government's policies. But with the fall of the Soviet Union, this sensitivity virtually disappeared from public representations of the period. After all, the intellectuals who failed to interfere with US Cold War policy indirectly facilitated an outcome that is now seen to be better than other possible outcomes. Moreover, had the intellectuals interfered with government policy, they might have prevented this outcome and helped to bring about a considerably worse state of affairs (e.g. Soviet domination). Therefore, with the

20/20 vision that only hindsight can afford, the intellectuals should perhaps not feel so guilty about their original political inaction. It takes only a small stretch of the historical imagination to convert what had been the intellectuals' calculated cowardice into their unconscious wisdom. Meanwhile, the political activists of the period appear as well-intentioned but, perhaps luckily, ineffectual. So much for negative responsibility!

At this point, some may argue that the elusiveness of negative responsibility merely highlights the inadequacy of an ethics based exclusively on evaluating the consequences of (actual or possible) actions. In that case, there is no safeguard that the moral significance of particular acts will not change over time, as their consequences interact with the consequences of other acts. Indeed, if the American hegemony should come to an end in the 21st century, those prudently inactive intellectuals from the 1960s may come to be judged as duplicitous cowards yet again! But this is an objection only if our moral judgements should be less corrigible than ordinary empirical judgements.

However, if we accept that our moral judgements should change as we learn more about what both preceded and followed particular acts, then there is nothing absurd about the presence of significant fluctuations in the moral status of acts and agents over time. In other words, it is *always* a matter for the future to decide whether we are heroes, villains or cowards. That relative agreement can be reached on the interim decisions simply reflects the relative agreement that exists over the causal structure of history, which, as Hegel clearly understood, is normally written from the standpoint of those for whom the past is a legacy they intend to take forward.

When a critic's understanding is at odds with that dominant in her time, she must construct an alternative counter-history, which typically involves the redistribution of praise, blame and significance across a wide range of agents, acts and events. These are what we earlier called Tory histories. They are often seen as 'revisionist'. They require considerable skill at juggling counter-factuals, especially ones relating to the sort of unactualised possibilities presupposed in the assignment of negative responsibility. The results are bound to be controversial in two senses. They challenge both received normative judgements about the past (and hence the legitimation they can offer the present) and received standards of evidence and inference, especially in terms of what may be inferred from the absence of evidence, either because it was never recorded or it has been subsequently suppressed.

Intellectual life turns out to be remarkably resilient to counter-historiography. While much is made of the difficulties of tracking the causal trajectory of ideas, these difficulties are more often invoked to shield intellectuals from the bad consequences of their ideas than to withdraw credit for their good consequences. Thus, scientists happily take responsibility for developments that enhance the human condition, even if they occurred several decades after the original intellectual innovation (e.g. Newton's responsibility for the Industrial Revolution), while distancing themselves from developments that diminish the human condition, even if they were brought about by the original intellectual innovators (e.g. the responsibility of the founders of modern atomic physics for nuclear weapons).

Even in these postmodern times, we still credit Locke with inspiring American democracy, as we continue to chastise those who would blame Nietzsche for seeding Nazism. In the case of Kuhn, the asymmetrical treatment may occur in the same body of work: philosophers of science chastise self-styled Kuhnians who read 'too much' relativism and political radicalism into his work, as they themselves fixate rather selectively on Kuhn's intermittent discussions of paradigms as conceptual exemplars for high praise and deep interpretation.

A good model for understanding the logic of this situation is provided by the sociology of Ibansk, the fictional USSR as recounted in Alexander Zinoviev's satirical novel, *The Yawning Heights*. The political theorist Jon Elster has identified 'three laws of Ibanskian sociology', which also applies to intellectuals. In my adaptation of these laws, I have replaced 'the leadership' with 'intellectuals':

1. People who want to make change end up changing nothing, while changes occur by those with no intention of making change.
2. Success is always due to intellectuals, even though intellectuals cannot bring it about deliberately.
3. Failure is always due to non-intellectuals, even though intellectuals may have unwittingly helped bring it about.

What is perhaps most noteworthy about these three laws is that they display a robust sense of negative responsibility, but only where the consequences of inaction are decidedly positive! The result is a style of historical writing whose vision is prospectively very weak but retrospectively very strong. (The Owl of Minerva may take flight only at dusk, but then it moves at the speed of light!) Moreover, intellectuals 'fail' only if the potential of their ideas remains unrealised. They never fail more straightforwardly, such as by having ideas that fail to measure up to reality. Thus, Hannah Arendt apologised for the Nazism of her old teacher-lover Heidegger by arguing that he failed to take his own ideas sufficiently seriously: he mistook the call of Hitler for that of *Logos*. As Max Weber might have put it, Heidegger's apparent failure in the 'ethics of responsibility' metamorphoses into a failure in the 'ethics of conviction'.

· CHAPTER 16 ·

FAILING THE POPPERIAN TEST FOR INTELLECTUAL RESPONSIBILITY: RORTY ON HEIDEGGER

You can be a great, original, and profound artist or thinker, and also a complete bastard.

Richard Rorty, 'Taking Philosophy Seriously'

A disturbing feature of 20th-century intellectual history is that the dominant figures of the two main European philosophical traditions – Ludwig Wittgenstein and Martin Heidegger – have promoted a conservative, even conformist, vision of social practice that accords an exaggerated metaphysical significance to sheer inertia. This is what Popper excoriated in science as 'induction' and in politics as 'historicism'. He went on to criticise Kuhn mainly on these grounds, as normal science is epitomised in the homely maxim: 'If the paradigm ain't broke, don't fix it.' But once Richard Rorty became a major interlocutor in the so-called 'conversation of mankind' with the publication of *Philosophy and the Mirror of Nature* in 1979, all of this was forgotten.

Rorty is the next best thing to a 'national philosopher' that the United States has produced since the heyday of William James and John Dewey almost a century ago. Rorty singles out his former Princeton colleague Thomas Kuhn for having shown that some vocabularies are so powerful that they change our relationship to the world. Thus Rorty glosses a Kuhnian scientific revolution. As for Popper, Rorty writes as if he had never existed – except in the essay from which the following passages are taken. Here Popper, perhaps the 20th-century philosopher most consistently hostile to epistemological foundationalism and 'essentialism' (a term he coined in *The Poverty of Historicism*), is made to appear as the very thing he opposed:

There is no way to correlate moral virtue with philosophical importance or philosophical doctrine. Being an original philosopher (and Heidegger was as original a philosopher as we have had in this century) is like being an original mathematician or an original microbiologist or consummate chess master: it is the result of some neural kink that occurs independently of other kinks. The only reason we think that good moral character is more important for professors of philosophy than for professors of other subjects is that we often use 'philosopher' as the name of an ideal human being: one who perfectly unites wisdom and kindness, insight and decency.

Still, even if we grant that philosophical talent and moral character swing free of each other, it is tempting to think that we can classify philosophies by reference to the moral or political message they convey ... Such attempts to simplify the thought of original thinkers ... should be avoided ... They are merely excuses for not reading them.

Karl Popper, in *The Open Society and Its Enemies*, did a good job of showing how passages in Plato, Hegel, and Marx could be taken to justify Hitlerian or Leninist takeovers, but to make his case he had to leave out 90 percent of each man's thought. [T]he works of anybody whose mind was complex enough to make his or her books worth reading will not have an 'essence,' [...] those books will admit of a fruitful diversity of interpretations, [...] the quest for 'an authentic reading' is pointless. One will assume that the author was as mixed-up as the rest of us, and that our job is to pull out, from the tangle we find on the pages, some lines of thought that might turn out to be useful for our own purposes.

These passages are central to the *cordon sanitaire* that Rorty erects between Heidegger's undeniable Nazism and Rorty's own view that Heidegger was the most original philosopher of the 20th century. Rorty does all he can to create maximum distance between the validity of what Rorty calls 'Heidegger's ideas' and both the origins and the consequences of those ideas – including the invocation of a far-fetched futuristic physiology. The rhetorical force of Rorty's argument is to make it seem as if the authoritarian roots and fruits of Heidegger's thought were a mere accident. To think otherwise, Rorty suggests, is itself to do an injustice to Heidegger's thought. These passages originally appeared in the 11 April 1988 edition of the US liberal weekly, *The New Republic*, under the title, 'Taking Philosophy Seriously'. But does it?

We have already seen that early reviewers of *The Structure of Scientific Revolutions* welcomed Kuhn's apparent turn away from positivism back to pragmatism. Rorty completes the turn. In so doing, he misses what drove the positivists, including Popper, to demonise the likes of Heidegger. Specifically, Rorty misses the spirit in which the distinction between the origins and the validity of ideas was originally drawn.

Nowadays, elementary logic instructors make much of the *genetic fallacy*, which is committed whenever someone infers the validity of an idea from its origins. However, it does not appear in Aristotle's original list of fallacies – probably because he did not regard it as one. The genetic fallacy was first identified in the 1934 edition of Morris Cohen and Ernest Nagel's *Introduction to Logic and the Scientific Method*, to counter crypto-racist claims that certain forms of knowledge are intrinsic to certain cultures, as in 'Jewish science' and 'Aryan science'. Such claims had been wide-spread among both natural and social scientists – both to praise and condemn – long before the Nazis turned it into a matter for state policy.

The genetic fallacy was also meant to popularise a distinction coined at roughly the same time by Popper and the logical positivist Hans Reichenbach between the *context of discovery* and the *context of justification*, the former concerning the origin and the latter the validity of scientific ideas. However, since Reichenbach's *Experience and Prediction* (1938) appeared in English long before Popper's *The Logic of Scientific Discovery*, Reichenbach is normally credited with canonising the distinction. Inter-estingly, he distinguished the contexts while enumerating the tasks of epistemology, which he listed in the following order: *description*, *criticism* and *advice*. In other words, one must first acquire a thorough understanding of the psychological and sociological factors surrounding a knowledge claim in order to see how its manner of presentation might affect the reception of its content. This is then subject to criticism, which results in a 'rational reconstruction' of the knowledge claim in a form that does not make reference to any potentially incriminating origins. Finally, some policy recommendation may be issued as to whether the claim should be believed, followed, etc.

A noteworthy feature of Reichenbach's epistemological procedure is that the context of discovery must be properly understood *before* the context of justification can be properly addressed. This point is not generally observed by philosophers today, especially those like Rorty who strain to prevent us from committing the genetic fallacy. Indeed, they so mis-recognise the genetic fallacy that they commit another fallacy in the process. Thus, Rorty takes the claim, 'The origins of an idea need not imply anything about its validity', to mean: 'The origins of an idea *never* imply anything about its validity.' This inferential slide is called the *modal fallacy*, whereby the modal operator 'not necessarily' (or 'need not') is read to mean 'necessarily not' (or 'never'). The import of committing the modal fallacy in this case is that Rorty preemptively closes inquiry on an issue that should be kept open until properly investigated.

The genetic fallacy is not designed to prohibit consideration of an idea's origins from an assessment of its validity. It has a more subtle function, namely, to shift the burden of proof to those who would claim that, say, Einstein's Jewish origins are *automatically* relevant to an evaluation of relativity theory. (This was a serious example at the time the fallacy was first raised.) These origins *may* be somehow relevant, but simply revealing them does not clinch the argument. Rather, one would need to go through the trouble of providing a causal account of exactly how Einstein's Jewish background predisposed him to propose a false physical theory that comes to be widely accepted only once others have been contaminated by the Jewish mindset.

Conversely, the *distinction* between the origins and the validity of an idea cannot be drawn simply as part of an ordinary reading of a published statement of the idea. On the contrary, we ordinarily import so many preconceptions into our reading that we blur the distinction, and hence unwittingly commit the genetic fallacy. For example, mass communications researchers have repeatedly shown that a message's credibility is strongly correlated with the receiver's knowledge of its source. The sheer fact that a text is required for a course or recommended by a learned friend already lowers one's critical guard to its content. As a safe-guard, then, we need to engage in some additional activity – be it logical translation, historical idealisation or science policy – that 'rationally reconstructs' the content of the published claim to knowledge.

But Rorty also wishes to sever the link between the validity of Heidegger's ideas and their *consequences*, especially their utility as Nazi ideology even without Heidegger's personal assistance. At this point, Rorty pays a visit to Ibansk, since as a self-confessed pragmatist he would normally judge the validity of an idea precisely by its consequences – except, so it seems, when they happen to be bad.

Rorty's Ibanskian turn reflects a deeper problem, namely, his profound lack of interest in the social conditions that have enabled Heidegger's thought to acquire their currency for us. Rorty merely assumes that if we find that Heidegger's master-work, *Being and Time*, addresses important problems in interesting ways, then we can reasonably con-clude that our response is not significantly related to either the book's origins or the process by which it came to be the text from which we seek guidance. Consequently, Rorty does not try to determine whether *Being and Time* speaks to us because the value of what it says transcends Heidegger's original context or simply because we have become unwitting captives to that context – victims of what I identified earlier as 'second-order colonialism': we would have allowed Heidegger's self-understanding to frame our own understanding of his work. For example, Rorty seems to share Heidegger's self-serving view that politics may occasionally 'realise' philosophy but is usually an interference that is best handled with utmost expedience. While this may help to explain the parameters within which Heidegger flirted with the Nazis, it fails to establish the distance needed for a critical evaluation of Heidegger's ideas.

A good way to capture the difference in attitude between Rorty and the positivists (including Popperians) on the validation of ideas is in terms of Paul Ricoeur's distinction between the *hermeneutics of trust and suspicion*. Thus, Rorty trusts the great philosophical texts as a benign legacy from which we freely fashion our own philosophical under-standings, while the more suspicious positivists and Popperians would first scrutinise the origins of all such texts before their messages can be properly identified and evaluated. This difference in attitude is traceable to at least two considerations. First, like many other intellectuals in the Weimar Republic, the positivists and Popper were critical of the self-certifying sense of immediacy conveyed by the emerging mass media, namely, radio and tabloid newspapers. This experience predisposed them to be sceptical about the reliability of idea transmission. Second, unlike Rorty, who regularly invokes the royal (hegemonic?) 'we' in his writings, the positivists and Popper never saw themselves as the designated heirs or intended recipients of prominent legacies. Rather, theirs was always a Tory's struggle to reclaim ground from the dominant 'irrationalist' tendencies of their day.

Rorty's insensitivity to second-order colonialism – our mental colonisation by other people's ideas – is also traceable to an effective dehumanisation of the texts he reads. Notwithstanding his periodic appeals to the 'conversation of mankind', Rorty treats texts not as repositories of intentions that may reach beyond the heads of their authors to shape readers' thoughts and actions, but as inert tools that have no ends of their own other than those provided by their users. Thus, Rorty worries only that we might fail to gain maximum advantage from *Being and Time* by taking its Nazi origins and consequences too seriously. He is not worried that such a text might do us maximum damage – say, by diverting us from goals that would truly serve our interests. Here Rorty reveals himself to be more pragmatist than hermeneutician.

Nevertheless, a schizoid feature of Rorty's position is that while he wants to detach the validity of

Heidegger's ideas from Heidegger's Nazi past, he still wants to credit those ideas as original to Heidegger, so that we continue to read *Being and Time*, as opposed to another book with similar content written by an anti-Nazi at roughly the same time. It is therefore crucial to Rorty's argument that *Being and Time*'s profundity be so great as to override the despicability of its author and the consequences to which he contributed – at least by not having tried to prevent and contain them, especially once the Nazis started to use Heidegger for legitimation. Is Rorty right that the nobility of Heidegger's life-project excuses his massive failure of negative responsibility?

The intuitive plausibility of Rorty's defence of Heidegger capitalises on historical memory to deform in a particular way. Memorability is tied to distinctiveness, which then tends to be read back as the essence of what is remembered. Thus, Heidegger is evaluated as a great philosopher who happened to be a Nazi, rather than a Nazi who happened to be a great philosopher. I shall dub this tendency the *haec ergo quid fallacy*. In ordinary English: 'My essence is defined by whatever distinguishes me from others.' This inference is fallacious for two reasons: first, distinctions among individuals may be superficial in relation to their underlying commonalities; second, and more relevant here, one's distinctiveness is an artefact of how the comparison with others is framed. In the case of Heidegger, then, we should ask if there were other philosophers of roughly the same vintage who said roughly the same things, but were not Nazis. If so, then the dispensation from negative responsibility urged by Rorty is not justified.

When I was first a student of philosophy 25 years ago, there were certainly just such non-Nazi alternatives to Heidegger. They included Karl Jaspers, Paul Tillich and Jean-Paul Sartre. Back then, Heidegger and they were routinely collected together as 'existentialists', and Heidegger would not necessarily have received the most respectful treatment. To be sure, there were important differences among these thinkers, but Rortyesque claims to Heidegger's 'striking originality' would certainly need to be tempered, if *Being and Time* continued to be read alongside *Reason and Existenz*, *The Courage to Be* and *Being and Nothingness*. In that case, one might reasonably query the source of the remaining philosophical nuances that distinguish Heidegger from these contemporaries, and the extent to which those nuances, if not altogether overvalued, might not be indebted to trains of thought that attracted Heidegger – but not Jaspers, Tillich or Sartre – to Nazism. This would make a good research project in the humanities, even today.

However, this question became difficult to pose once 'existentialism' disappeared as the name of a philosophical school, along with sustained study of its major proponents – except, of course, Heidegger. He was renovated as a seminal transition figure: the final deconstructive moment of a larger and older school, 'phenomenology', which seeded the current waves of postmodern continental European thought. Moreover, unlike his existentialist rivals, the disruption of Heidegger's academic career by World War II never forced a major reorientation of his thought in relation to new audiences. As the trajectories of philosophy, psychology, theology and literature moved farther apart, the impact of Jaspers, Tillich and Sartre became more disparate.

Ironically, Heidegger's intellectual stature may have even been *helped* by the time-honoured practice of 'learning from the opponent' in which victors indulge after a war. In this respect, Heidegger's political 'genius' may lie in having stuck with the Nazis long enough for the Americans to discover him during De-Nazification without ending up being judged an untouchable war criminal whose works had to be banned. As committed anti-Nazis ensconced in Allied countries, Heidegger's existentialist rivals never underwent such intense scrutiny nor subsequently acquired such a mystique for depth and danger. These facts, combined with an aggressive placement of disciples in academic posts (not least Hans-Georg Gadamer), have contributed to the image of Heidegger as someone engaged in a 'life project' that probed more widely and deeply than his rivals' worthy but more disparate inquiries.

Questions about the relative depth of Heidegger's philosophical project are certainly possible, and even desirable, given that greater recognition of Heidegger's singular 'genius' has historically coincided with greater awareness of his Nazi past. It is easy to imagine a considered judgement by future intellectual historians that might today be regarded as cynical: 'The status of Heidegger's philosophy was artificially magnified in the late 20th century to avoid having to face the full normative implications of a "life of the mind" so radically detached from the concerns of ordinary humanity.' I believe something similar may be worth saying about Kuhn's status.

· CHAPTER 17 ·

IS THOMAS KUHN THE AMERICAN HEIDEGGER?

I remember being invited to a seminar at Princeton organized by undergraduates during the [1968 student revolts]. *And I kept saying, 'But I didn't say that! But I didn't say that! But I didn't say that!' And finally, a student of mine … said to the students, 'You have to realize that in terms of what you are thinking of, this is a profoundly conservative book'. And it is; I mean, in the sense that I was trying to explain how it could be that the most rigid of all disciplines, and in certain circumstances the most authoritarian, could also be the most creative of novelty.*

Thomas Kuhn, from his last major interview
(1995), reprinted in *The Road since Structure*

The recipe [for a successful science], *according to* [Kuhn's social science followers], *is to restrict criticism, to reduce the number of comprehensive theories to one, and to create a normal science that has this one theory as its paradigm. Students must be prevented from speculating along different lines* *and the more restless colleagues must be made to conform and 'to do serious work'. **Is this what Kuhn wants to achieve?** Is it his intention to provide a historico-scientific justification for the ever growing need to identify with some group?*

Paul Feyerabend, 'Consolations
for the Specialist'

There are some disconcerting similarities between the reception of Heidegger and Kuhn. One concerns the gradual upgrading of their main works as literary achievements after initial censure from professional philosophers, especially in the English-speaking world. *Being and Time*, rushed into print in support of Heidegger's professorship, was for many years regarded as the paradigm case of incoherence. Heideggerian pronouncements, such as 'Nothing negates', provided the logical positivists with endless examples of what Wittgenstein dubbed 'language on holiday', the source of mystification and illegitimate authority in society at large. Similarly, for perhaps its first ten years, Kuhn's *Structure* was derided by the positivists' Anglophone offspring, analytic philosophers of science, for its amateurism and ambiguities. Thus, Margaret Masterman notoriously recorded 23 distinct meanings of 'paradigm' in the first edition of *Structure* alone. Yet, as subsequent generations of philosophers came to rely on Heidegger or Kuhn as the basis for their own work, these original liabilities have come to be seen as marks of the 'semantically rich' and 'open-textured' nature of their books.

Indeed, the original liabilities have been converted into intellectual strengths, a phenomenon that Jon Elster usefully calls 'sweet lemons' (the mirror image of 'sour grapes'). Heidegger continues to be given credit for stretching the limits of language in a worthy attempt to grasp the nature of Being, whereas Kuhn's lack of philosophical finesse has not hurt his reputation. On the contrary, the significance of philosophical expertise has itself declined in the science studies disciplines. Formal philosophical training, while not completely disregarded, has come to be seen as an illegitimate substitute for an immersion in specific scientific practices. Whether this immersion should occur via formal scientific training or participant-observation at research sites is the main point of contention between the naturalist philosophers and constructivist sociologists who vie for Kuhn's legacy today in science studies.

But perhaps the clearest institutional sign of philosophy's decline in the understanding of science is the gradual incorporation of the field of 'history and philosophy of science' into a more generic 'science studies'. In the former field, Kuhn is given roughly equal treatment alongside his contemporaries, Lakatos, Feyerabend, Stephen Toulmin and Norwood Russell Hanson. Each was sensitive to the role of historicity, paradigmaticity, sociality and incommensurability in science. However, Kuhn surges ahead as a mythical father figure in science studies. Recalling the analogy to Heidegger, the disappearance of history and philosophy of science is akin to the disappearance of existentialism, and Kuhn's status in science studies is comparable to Heidegger's in postmodern philosophy.

To be sure, there is this one difference between Heidegger and Kuhn: while Heidegger was reabsorbed into phenomenology as its most profound contributor before being made the key transition figure to postmodernism, Kuhn was reabsorbed, more fully and generically, as a naïve exemplar of any of several philosophical positions – relativism, Kantianism, Wittgensteinianism, naturalism, pragmatism – which is then treated as the source of whatever one takes to be the conceptual strengths or weaknesses of contemporary science studies.

From a Popperian standpoint, the first question to ask about the parallel trajectories of Heidegger and Kuhn is why they – and not the relevant alternative contemporaries – have come to acquire such massive significance in their respective fields, especially given that neither Heidegger nor Kuhn nor their partisans ever answered the original criticisms of their work. To respond to this query simply by appealing to the luminous nature of their ideas is disingenuous on two grounds.

First, the realisation of this 'luminosity' tracks the historical rise in the ideas' popularity too closely to function as an independent measure of the ideas' true significance. Once Heidegger and Kuhn came to legitimate a large body of intellectual work, there is little wonder that their ideas would be treated as luminous: even academics know better than to saw off the limb of the tree on which they sit. The second and related issue is that confidence in Heidegger's and Kuhn's luminosity tends to vary inversely with one's knowledge of work by the relevant alternative contemporaries. Thus, younger researchers are much more likely than older ones to call Kuhn or Heidegger a 'genius'. Moreover, the luminous progenitor is credited with having originated such banalities as Kuhn's 'discovery' that 'science is problem-solving', something common to a wide range of less celebrated thinkers who may also have other virtues that the progenitor lacks. As Orwell – and Kuhn – would have it, historical amnesia does wonders to focus the collective mind.

The above pattern of response is familiar from the annals of cross-cultural rationality – though normally it is associated with the superstitious beliefs of primitive tribes. For example, anthropologists have no problem demonstrating the socially stabilising function of rain dances, given the vast symbolic structures that have been erected around these rituals. The 'irrationality' of such practices, however, lies in their continuation even after the natives learn that the dances are at best accidentally connected to anything that might reliably bring about rain. In other words, the natives fixate on the rain dance itself rather than shift their attention to other practices that might better achieve what the rain dance sets out to do. When Popperian anthropologists like Ernest Gellner and Ian Jarvie first made these observations in the 1960s, they were criticised for harbouring the Western assumption that a rain dance has value only as a means for bringing about, or at least predicting, rain. On the contrary, it was argued, the dance's primary value may be precisely its integrative force in the society practising it, which in turn explains why the natives are wise not to question its foundations, as the Popperians would have them do.

Whatever one wishes to make of this response to the Popperians, it would be odd if we were forced to say something similar in the case of today's Heideggerian and Kuhnian rain dances. After all, as we saw in Rorty's protestations against evaluating ideas by their origins and consequences, those who take seriously Heidegger's and Kuhn's ideas claim to do so because of the light those ideas shed on a chosen aspect of reality. In that case, the Popperian concern with measuring up the means against the ends they purport to serve would seem to be especially apposite, perhaps more so than in the case of the native rain dances. Thus, we may ask: are Kuhn's ideas sufficiently powerful for understanding the nature of science to justify the disproportionate attention given to them? If, after a comparison with the ideas of relevant alternatives (e.g. Feyerabend, Lakatos, Toulmin, Hanson), the answer turns out to be no, then we need to find out why Kuhn has nevertheless received such attention. The hint of irrationality in the mass adoption of Kuhn is heightened by Kuhn's own failure to participate in – and, if anything, to disavow – the spread of the ideas associated with him.

At the very least, Kuhn's reclusiveness goes against the sense of social responsibility that intellectuals have traditionally felt for their work. While it is quite natural for people to feel responsible for their actions, which of course are informed by ideas, the mark of the intellectual is to believe that ideas themselves have consequences for which one is then responsible once they are published. Here Kuhn is usefully contrasted with Michel Foucault, whose work was also subject to rather rapid and disparate adoption at roughly the same period, indeed sometimes (at least in the Anglophone world) alongside Kuhn's work. However, unlike Kuhn, who increasingly withdrew from discussions of his work as it became more popular, Foucault spent considerable effort, typically in interviews, elucidating his background assumptions and engaging with the normative implications that both his fans and critics had drawn from his work. Indeed, Foucault provides a model of an intellectual who tried to classify the sorts of political activities that could and could not be supported by his words.

Interestingly, Kuhn and Foucault agreed that it was impossible to write a history of the recent past. Yet, Foucault had no problem using his pre-20th-century 'histories of the present' as a basis for contemporary critical intervention. This was because Kuhn and Foucault had rather different grounds for believing in the impossibility of contemporary history. While Kuhn believed that archival material relating to the recent history of science could be organised – indeed, he led such an activity for the American Physical Society in the

1960s – he did not believe that a proper history could be written as long as the major intellectual issues were still unresolved. In line with the incommensurability thesis, Kuhn believed that history requires that the past be treated as a foreign land, separated in time as if by space. In contrast, Foucault's doubts about the writing of recent history were based on the historian's lack of authority in speaking for evidence that is still being used to legitimate contemporary regimes. Instead, Foucault believed that his 'counter-hegemonic' strategy of marrying the 'specialised erudition' of the library and archives with the 'subjugated knowledges' of the dispossessed resembled the sort of power that marginalised aristocrats could exercise on behalf of the poor in bourgeois societies.

When comparing the responses of Kuhn and Foucault, it is worth noting that by the time they had to account for the consequences of their ideas, both held prestigious and secure academic posts. Neither had to worry about the impact of their responses on their livelihood. In that respect, both were burdened with significant negative responsibility, but only Foucault rose to the challenge.

In Kuhn's defence, it might be said that since the end of World War II, France's public intellectual culture has been much stronger than America's. Yet, Kuhn declined many opportunities for engagement, even from academic colleagues, especially Paul Feyerabend, who had read *Structure* in draft, taught the finished product at Berkeley, and wrote Kuhn several detailed and pointed letters around the theme of *Structure* as 'ideology covered up as history' – to which Kuhn never gave an adequate response, even after Feyerabend published the paper as 'Consolations for the Specialist' in the follow-up volume to Lakatos' 1965 conference.

Very unlike Foucault, Kuhn's pattern of written communication reveals someone who responded generously only to those few who read his work as he himself did. Perhaps the most notable exception is a three-month exchange with the US sociologist Jessie Bernard in 1969–70, in which she managed to engage Kuhn on the competing demands from 'the establishment' and 'the movement' on the natural sciences. Here Kuhn remarked that natural scientists, unlike social scientists, were unlikely to allow such external pressures to reorient their research significantly. On the contrary, Kuhn believed they might even become more focused on their normal puzzle-solving activities. This certainly described Kuhn's response to his own similar situation.

Given Kuhn's studied distance from the ideas invoked in his name, it is reasonable to suppose that, as in the case of Heidegger, proximity to the world-historic spirit has played a much stronger role in the conveyance of Kuhnian ideas than we care to admit. The Minutes of the Committee on General Education make clear that Kuhn was denied tenure at Harvard because, as of late 1955, he seemed to have accomplished little on his own that was not beholden to James Bryant Conant, who had recently stepped down from the university's presidency to become the first US ambassador to West Germany. Moreover, Kuhn's debt to Conant appears to have persisted throughout his career, since even in his final interview Kuhn deemed Conant the brightest person he had ever met. This makes Kuhn a difficult case for the critique of intellectuals. For while Kuhn clearly benefited from Conant's patronage, Conant never asked Kuhn to do anything that he was unwilling to do. Perhaps because Kuhn's reliance on Conant was so *exclusive*, there are none of the traces of resistance that normally help to clarify the extent of an intellectual's dependency on the powers that be.

Overall, the Conant–Kuhn relationship is best characterised as an exchange in which each used the other for his own ends. The looming normative question is whether each considered why the other would want to use him as he did. By his own account, Conant was largely responsible for introducing the industrial division of labour model of scientific research from German to American academia in the 1920s, as chairman of the Harvard chemistry department. Conant was also fully aware that many excellent students like Kuhn who underwent scientific training at the start of World War II to pursue philosophical questions by low-tech means would be disappointed by the scaled-up specialised work of 'Big Science' that awaited them at the end of the war. The General Education in Science programme was created with them specific-ally in mind. There they could impart to students a vision of science that focused on self-directed cognitive change, with science's political-economic entanglements playing a distinctly secondary role. Conant reasoned that the more future policy-makers could see the hand of Maxwell or Einstein in an expensive and risky research project, the more likely science's autonomy would be preserved in its increasing involvements in the Cold War's military-industrial complex.

Kuhn, of course, wanted to promote much the same vision as Conant, but mainly because it captured his original reason for pursuing science as natural philosophy by more exact means. More-over, Conant and Kuhn overlapped not only in their overall vision of science but also in at least one means of realising that vision, namely, the manufacture of student course materials to bring out what is now often called the 'internal' history of science. Thus, a selection of original scientific works were edited for student consumption by foregrounding their cognitive content and eliminating, or reducing to annotation, the background political-economic-cultural context that made those works meaningful to their original readers. The results were the influential *Harvard Case Histories in Experimental Science* (1950). What neither Conant nor Kuhn anticipated, or approved, was that their shared non-instrumental vision of science would be appropriated by humanists and social scientists, in part to relativise the nature of science to whatever a community of inquirers happens to agree as their 'paradigm'.

Just as we must distinguish Conant's intellectual responsibility from Kuhn's, we must also distinguish Kuhn's intellectual responsibility from that of his uncritical readers. And we must distinguish between the validity of Conant's political realism and the validity of Kuhn's passive acceptance of Conant's political realism. To be sure, it was because Conant's actions were bound by his secular responsibilities that Kuhn managed to enjoy the measure of intellectual freedom that he did at Harvard. But it is possible that Conant made the best of a bad situation, without Kuhn thereby being excused for having failed to question the basis of

Conant's strategy. As a benchmark, consider Noam Chomsky, who was awarded an endowed professorship at MIT when that university's influence on US Cold War policy was at its peak. Yet, Chomsky had no problem biting the hand that fed him. In contrast, Kuhn remained silent, even once he was tenured first at Princeton and later at MIT, as himself a holder of an endowed chair.

Kuhn was content not to question the larger context in which his work figured as long as it allowed him to do what he wanted. In the Cold War, this 'heads-down' posture was typical of scientists who worked under military contracts: they were allowed considerable day-to-day freedom of inquiry, as long as they obtained security clearance before publication and did not question the uses to which funders put their research. With the Manhattan Project's success in constructing the first atomic bomb with minimum external oversight, the US government came to be persuaded of the value of scientific self-governance. Indeed, this fact convinced Conant that science would not be deformed by military funding. The fruits have included the foundations of the most distinctive developments in the non-natural sciences in the second half of the 20th century: game theory, decision theory, artificial intelligence, cybernetics, operations research and cognitive science – not to mention the analytic philosophy that explicates and legitimates this work.

In practice, the need for security clearance rarely posed a problem to research publications in these areas because their abstract and specialised nature impinged only very indirectly on national defence concerns. Problems arose only once a scientist decided to take an interest in the ends pursued by those on whom her autonomy depended, perhaps because she had come to believe that everyone lives in the same moral universe and hence should abide by the same principles. One prominent example was the scandal associated with *The Pentagon Papers*, classified documents about the Vietnam War that were passed to the *New York Times* in 1971 by the prominent decision theorist, Daniel Ellsberg. However, Kuhn was never in danger of crossing that line.

Kuhn undoubtedly understood the different social functions that science might perform, but he deliberately chose to dwell on only one of them – its function as organised inquiry. In a 1990 interview with an alumni publication, the *Harvard Science Review*, Kuhn justified this decision, when asked why he had not altered his account in the light of 20th-century developments in science. He suggested that at some point in its history, the principal social function of science may turn (or have turned) out to be a factor of production or an instrument of governance, rather than a search for knowledge. At that point, science drops out of the normative horizons of Kuhn's model. While science might continue to produce truths on a reliable basis, the truths so produced would be done under social conditions that prevent science from simply following the logic of its own paradigm, which is ultimately what the search for knowledge is all about.

Thus, Kuhn was alive to the difference between pursuing knowledge as *an end in itself* and as a *prerequisite for pursuing other ends*. The former captures Kuhn's own sensibility, the latter Conant's, though together they defined the 'serving two masters' mentality that enabled scientists to thrive in the Cold War environment. In this respect, 'autonomous inquirer' and 'organisation man' could co-exist as two separate aspects of the same person – that is, unless one was, say, Daniel Ellsberg. Indeed, the Kuhnian normal scientist was the model for just such a person.

This sensitivity gave Kuhn a distinct rhetorical advantage over his Popperian and positivist rivals. In effect, he was much more the ventriloquist than they. It was not, as is often said, that Kuhn was more 'descriptive' and his rivals more 'prescriptive' with respect to the history of science. The Popperians especially were no less learned in the history of the physical sciences than Kuhn, but they insisted on imposing their normative perspective on that history, and hence appeared perversely contrarian to a public for whom the authority of science was self-evident. In contrast, Kuhn let his normative orientation speak through the skew and arrangement of his historical examples: he included that which he approved and omitted that which he did not – but he never articulated the norm that underwrote his decisions. Thus, the careful reader is simply left to infer why Kuhn chose to omit, say, the history of chemistry after the 1850s and the history of physics after the 1920s. Given Kuhn's exclusive interest in science as pure inquiry, it is reasonable to conclude that he believed that after those dates, those disciplines ceased to be relevant to his model, presumably because their secular entanglements irrevocably distorted the course of their inquiries. But at the same time, Kuhn equally thought that he had no business issuing these judgements in the public domain, especially as *Structure* became a campus best-seller in the turbulent late 1960s.

However, it would be a mistake to conclude that Kuhn originally set out to write *The Structure of Scientific Revolutions* as a doubly encoded text, deliberately masking its relevance to contemporary science. Rather, the present only gradually receded from view in Kuhn's writing. Early drafts of *Structure*, from the late 1950s, contain undeveloped references to Darwin and Freud that were excised from the final version. Earlier still, as an instructor in General Education (letter dated 2 December 1952), Kuhn was invited by Conant's positivist-in-residence, Philipp Frank, to participate in a project he was organising with Ernest Nagel on the 'sociology of science'. It was to be oriented toward understanding how science's professional structures both facilitate and inhibit theory testing. Kuhn drafted a letter in response (which remained unsent) outlining what was to become his theory of paradigms. In particular, Kuhn took issue with the idea that professional structures somehow existed in tension with scientific work, since he regarded such structures as the very embodiment of scientific norms, going so far as to claim that they have replaced metaphysics and faith as the foundations of science in the 20th century. It is striking that an observation so clearly made about contemporary science will be read back into the entire history of science in *Structure*.

Indeed, if proof were needed that our minds have been colonised by Kuhn's image of science, we would need look no further than our uncritical acceptance of Kuhn's blatantly *syncretistic* approach to history. 'Syncretism' is the superimposition of features from two or more historical periods, which often serves to remove any sense that substantial change has occurred in the interim. Thus, Kuhn's influential conceptual apparatus – epitomised in phrases like 'normal science', 'puzzle solving', 'mopping up operations' – echoes scientific research done in a scaled-up, industrialised mode, which really came into its own in the aftermath of World War I, that is, the period immediately *after* that from which most of Kuhn's historical examples are taken. (To their credit, Popperians have consistently questioned this feature of Kuhn's historiography.) At stake here are the background social conditions under which science is regarded as a self-organising community of inquirers with sufficient control over the means of knowledge production to enjoy sovereignty over who counts as a scientist, what counts as a valid knowledge claim and an appropriate research direction. Kuhn's syncretism leaves the historically mistaken – but, in the Cold War context, ideologically palatable – impression that hyper-specialisation is the price that scientists have *always* had to pay to ensure the autonomy of their inquiries.

Moreover, not only did Kuhn think it was not his business to criticise contemporary science for failing to adhere to the norms of pure inquiry, but he also thought that no one else should use his work for that purpose. Case in point is Jerome Ravetz, author of the most systematic attempt to develop a critical theory out of Kuhn's theory of science: *Scientific Knowledge and Its Social Problems*, published by Oxford University Press in 1971. Ravetz, an American expatriate who helped to spearhead the British Society for Social Responsibility in Science in the 1970s, corresponded with Kuhn for three decades, initially over their common interest in the Copernican Revolution. However, as time went on, Kuhn became increasingly uncomfortable with Ravetz's political interests and activities, though Ravetz continued to call upon Kuhn for advice and letters of recommendation. For example, in a letter to Ravetz (21 June 1972), Kuhn claimed not to like the final hundred pages of Ravetz's book, in which he enunciates a programme for 'critical science', aligned with Barry Commoner's ecology movement. Today, Ravetz's critical science is notable for its pioneering discussion of research ethics and intellectual property. Yet, five years after expressing his misgivings, Kuhn wrote, unbeknownst to Ravetz, against hiring him as professor in history and sociology of science at the University of Pennsylvania on the grounds that Ravetz had left scholarship behind for politics (letter to Arnold Thackray, 7 April 1977).

I have already raised the examples of Chomsky, Ellsberg and Foucault as contemporaries of Kuhn who, in their rather different ways, took responsibility for the ideas they produced. It is worth remarking that this view was also shared by those whose theories of science were most similar to Kuhn's. Thus, Kuhn's conspicuous silence on the politics of science in the 1960s and 70s may be contrasted with the following public interventions by philosophers of science:

- At the height of the Vietnam War, Karl Popper called for scientists to adopt a version of the Hippocratic Oath to restrain their propensity for harm.

- Imre Lakatos claimed that particle physics constituted a 'degenerating problem-shift' that was propped up only because its ever more powerful computers and atom smashers served the military-industrial complex.

- Paul Feyerabend advocated the devolution of science funding from nation-states to local communities as the surest way to increase science's capacity for good and lower its capacity for evil.

- Stephen Toulmin argued (against Michael Polanyi) that science had lost any unity of identity and purpose as it became integral to the processes of governance and wealth production.

This list is interesting because, despite their overlapping theoretical interests, these philosophers varied considerably across the ideological spectrum. Specifically, they did not all stand on the political left, yet they felt compelled to speak out against the deformation of science in their times.

Given the success of *Structure*, Kuhn was better positioned than his contemporaries to make an intervention that would have given some focus and clarity to the inchoate critiques of science in society at large. Of course, several reasons may be offered for Kuhn's silence. Most of these reasons do not speak well to his courage, his concern, his clarity of mind or his sense of the times. But in the end, there remains the original objection to negative responsibility that would cast Kuhn's inaction in a more favourable light: the integrity of his life-project was more important than the difference his critical intervention would have made. Indeed, Kuhn should perhaps, then, be congratulated for not allowing his vision to be clouded by quotidian events, which could have dissipated his efforts.

I close with two comments on this interpretation of Kuhn's inaction. First, as in the case of Heidegger, attempts to exonerate Kuhn become increasingly self-serving over time, since *we* are the primary beneficiaries of Kuhn's life-project, and as time goes on, our own life-projects, unsurprisingly, depart from Kuhn's. Excusing Kuhn thus becomes a covert way of justifying ourselves. Second, the bare fact that Kuhn, again like Heidegger, requires special dispensation from negative responsibility does not speak well about the times in which he lived. Heidegger's defenders derive considerable rhetorical support from an image of Nazi Germany as so oppressive that it could deform so profound a thinker as Heidegger. Is perhaps some similar argument about Cold War America required to add moral ballast to Kuhn's silence? The lack of such an argument to date suggests that we have yet to assess the full moral cost of claiming that Kuhn flourished in – and not in spite of – Cold War America.

FURTHER READING

Kuhn and Popper related to their texts rather differently, but both wrote with a surface clarity that masked considerable ambiguity, inconsistency and shifts in position over time.

Kuhn's first book, *The Copernican Revolution* (Chicago: University of Chicago Press, 1957), was a work of synthetic history that struck readers at the time as a decent textbook, despite its lack of original scholarship. Kuhn's subsequent success has led to a retrospective upgrading of its significance. Kuhn's immense public reputation rests almost entirely on his second book, *The Structure of Scientific Revolutions* (Chicago: University of Chicago Press, 1962). Most commentators rely on the second edition (1970), where Kuhn begins a bewildering tendency to retreat from any radical-sounding claims. Kuhn's only subsequent monograph was a technically accomplished but intellectually unadventurous account of the origins of quantum mechanics: *Black Body Radiation and Quantum Discontinuity: 1894–1912* (Oxford: Clarendon Press,

1978). Kuhn's historiographical essays are compiled in *The Essential Tension* (Chicago: University of Chicago Press, 1977), and his later, more analytic-philosophical work is brought together in *The Road since Structure* (Chicago: University of Chicago Press, 2000). This book also contains Kuhn's last major interview, which brings out nicely Kuhn's ambivalent self-understanding as, on the one hand, a misunderstood genius and, on the other, a lucky amateur. Notably, the book was edited by James Bryant Conant's grandson, a Harvard-trained philosopher who has been appointed Kuhn's literary executor. Up to the time of his death from cancer in 1996, Kuhn had been working on a book-length follow-up to *Structure*, which J.B.C. III may someday bring into print.

Popper, more than he cared to admit, remained very 'German' in regarding his work as a living corpus – a 'life-project' – that was under constant revision. Consequently, there are several versions of most of Popper's major writings, all of which are now available from Routledge. Most English readers first became acquainted with Popper's works on political theory and philosophy of the social sciences, especially *The Open Society and Its Enemies* (London: Routledge, 1945) and *The Poverty of Historicism* (London: Routledge, 1957), both written in the 1940s and with fascism in view. However, as

Popper's reputation was consolidated in the 1950s, they came to be read more as anti-Communist tracts, all without the benefit of Popper's underlying epistemological views. Indeed, before Popper translated an expanded version of *The Logic of Scientific Discovery* (London: Hutchinson, 1959) into English, his philosophy of science had been confined to either technical philosophical journals or, interestingly, radio talks and other popular venues. These pieces were collected together as *Conjectures and Refutations* (London: Routledge, 1963), which was followed by *Objective Knowledge* (Oxford: Oxford University Press, 1972), a more metaphysically inspired work that attempts to treat knowledge as a single type of thing that applies to multiple realms of being. In *Unended Quest: An Intellectual Autobiography* (London: Fontana, 1976), Popper settles some old scores. In recent years, Routledge has been steadily publishing thematic collections of Popper's occasional pieces. The two volumes that are most relevant to the issues raised in this book are *The Myth of the Framework* (London: Routledge, 1994) and *Lesson of this Century* (London: Routledge, 1997).

Both Kuhn and Popper have been somewhat overdue in receiving book-length critical treatments of their bodies of work. However, over the last decade, the pace of publication has quickened.

Rather than listing many texts of variable quality, I shall recommend the ones that I believe their subjects would have liked the most: Paul Hoyningen-Huene, *Reconstructing Scientific Revolutions: Thomas S. Kuhn's Philosophy of Science* (Chicago: University of Chicago Press, 1993); Mark Notturno, *Science and the Open Society: The Future of Karl Popper's Philosophy* (Budapest: Central European University Press, 1999).

The archives of Kuhn and Popper are readily available to scholars. Popper's are at the Hoover Institution, a right-wing think-tank on the Stanford University campus. Kuhn's are at the MIT Special Collections for former faculty members. I have also found useful the Harvard-based Presidential Papers of James Bryant Conant and the Minutes of the Committee on General Education.

In 2000, two books were published that took advantage of the archival material, as well as published sources: Steve Fuller, *Thomas Kuhn: A Philosophical History for Our Times* (Chicago: University of Chicago Press, 2000) and Malachi Hacohen, *Karl Popper: The Formative Years, 1902–1945* (Cambridge: Cambridge University Press, 2000). Although Hacohen and I worked in ignorance of each other, we managed to produce complementary works: Popper turns out to be more beholden to the political left and Kuhn to the political right than popular mythology would have. The first port of call for queries about the details in this book should be these two books and a third, John Kadvany, *Imre Lakatos and the Guises of Reason* (Durham: Duke University Press, 2001).

All the final versions of the papers from the original Kuhn–Popper encounter are compiled in *Criticism and the Growth of Knowledge,* eds Imre Lakatos and Alan Musgrave (Cambridge: Cambridge University Press, 1970). Another inspired collection of related texts is *Scientific Revolutions*, ed. Ian Hacking (Oxford: Oxford University Press, 1981). It includes Dudley Shapere's 'Meaning and Scientific Change', an early systematic attempt to integrate Kuhn's *Structure* into mainstream philosophy of science, Popper's 'The Rationality of Scientific Revolutions', Lakatos' 'History of Science and Its Rational Reconstructions' and Feyerabend's 'How to Defend Society against Science'. Also worth consulting is the Lakatos–Feyerabend correspondence from 1968 to 1974, which reveals the academic and real-world politics that fuelled their philosophical imaginations: Imre Lakatos and Paul Feyerabend, *For and Against Method*, ed. Matteo Motterlini (Chicago: University of Chicago Press, 1999). This book also usefully includes a transcribed version of the last set of Lakatos' undergraduate lectures. Readers who do not recall the 'received view' in the philosophy of science that both Kuhn and Popper were sometimes credited with having overthrown should look at the last major American statement of logical positivism, Ernest Nagel, *The Structure of Science* (New York: Routledge, 1961), alongside the volume that formally marked the passing of the received view: *The Structure of Scientific Theories*, ed. Fred Suppe (Urbana: University of Illinois Press, 1977).

The idea that philosophy of science is a second-order spin-out of substantive debates in the sciences replays a theme in the history of philosophy more generally, one that has been systematically pursued in Randall Collins, *The Sociology of Philosophies: A Global Theory of Intellectual Change* (Cambridge: Harvard University Press, 1998). The book is an excellent source on the institutional relationships between philosophy and the special sciences, as well as the importance of the university as a vehicle of collective inquiry down through the ages. In the case of the United States, especially Harvard, see Bruce Kuklick, *The History of Philosophy in America, 1720–2000* (Oxford: Oxford University Press, 2001). In the case of Germany, see Fritz Ringer, *The Decline of the German Mandarins* (Cambridge: Harvard University Press, 1969); Herbert Schnaedelbach, *Philosophy in Germany, 1831–1933* (Cambridge: Cambridge University Press, 1984). A good sense of the Viennese inter-war culture that spawned Popper and the logical positivists may be gained from David Edmonds and John Eidinow, *Wittgenstein's Poker: The Story of a Ten-Minute Argument between Two Great Philosophers* (London: Faber and Faber, 2001). Kuhn's mentor, James Bryant Conant, wrote a thorough autobiography, *My Several Lives: Memoirs of a Social Inventor* (New York: Harper and Row, 1970), and is subject to an equally thorough biography: James Hershberg, *James B. Conant: Harvard to Hiroshima and the Making of the Nuclear Age* (New York: Alfred Knopf, 1993). Together they provide a panoramic sweep of science, politics and the academy as seen from a key gatekeeper in Cold War America. The hand of Kuhn in recent European science policy thinking may be felt in Michael Gibbons et al, *The New Production of Knowledge* (London: Sage, 1994).

Some more specialised historical works may be recommended to fill in the details: Cyril Barrett, 'Believing in order to understand', in *Verstehen and Humane Understanding*, ed. Anthony O'Hear (Cambridge: Cambridge University Press, 1996), pp. 223–34; J. Peter Euben, 'Corruption', in *Political Innovation and Conceptual Change*, eds T. Ball, J. Farr, R. Hanson (Cambridge: Cambridge University Press, 1989), chapter 11; Gillian Evans, *A Brief History of Heresy* (Oxford: Blackwell, 2003); James

Franklin, *The Science of Conjecture* (Baltimore: Johns Hopkins University Press, 2001); Ian Hacking, *The Emergence of Probability* (Cambridge: Cambridge University Press, 1975); Paul Hoyningen-Huene, 'Two Letters of Paul Feyerabend to Thomas Kuhn on a Draft of *The Structure of Scientific Revolutions*', *Studies in History and Philosophy of Science* 26 (1995), pp. 353–88; Ian Jarvie, *The Republic of Science: The Emergence of Popper's Social View of Science, 1935–1945* (Amsterdam: Rodopi, 2001); Larry Laudan, *Science and Hypothesis* (Dordrecht: Kluwer, 1981); *Origins of Logical Empiricism*, eds Ronald Giere and Alan Richardson (Minneapolis: University of Minnesota Press, 1996); George Reisch, 'Did Kuhn Kill Logical Empiricism?', *Philosophy of Science* 58 (1991), pp. 264–77; Martin Roiser and Carla Willig, 'The Strange Death of the Authoritarian Personality', *History of the Human Sciences* 15 (2002), 4, pp. 71–96; Michael Ruse, *Mystery of Mysteries: Is Evolution a Social Construction?* (Cambridge: Harvard University Press, 1999); Skuli Sigurdsson, 'The Nature of Scientific Knowledge: An Interview with Thomas Kuhn', *Harvard Science Review*, Winter 1990, pp. 18–25; Barry Smith, *Austrian Philosophy: The Legacy of Franz Brentano* (La Salle: Open Court Press, 1994); V. Betty Smocovitis, *Unifying Biology: The Evolutionary Synthesis and Evolutionary Biology* (Princeton: Princeton University Press, 1996);

R. Steven Turner, 'Paradigms and Productivity', *Social Studies of Science* 17 (1987), pp. 35–68.

Perhaps the most influential – and misguided – attempt to turn Kuhn into a radical thinker appears in Part Three of Richard Rorty, *Philosophy and the Mirror of Nature* (Princeton: Princeton University Press, 1979). The dubious honour of misapplying Kuhn to legitimate the social sciences must go to Charles Taylor, 'Interpretation and the Sciences of Man', *Review of Metaphysics* 25 (1971), pp. 3–51. On how Kuhn has changed the philosophy of science by making it much more 'philosophy *for* science', see *Taking the Naturalistic Turn, or How Real Philosophy of Science is Done*, ed. Werner Callebaut (Chicago: University of Chicago Press, 1993), a creative and revealing set of interviews; *The Disunity of Science*, eds Peter Galison and David Stump (Stanford: Stanford University Press, 1996), a representative anthology of post-Kuhnian science studies; Ian Hacking, *Representing and Intervening* (Cambridge: Cambridge University Press, 1983), still the best textbook capturing this sensibility as a break from earlier philosophy of science. Perhaps the most publicly successful post-Kuhnian has been Philip Kitcher, a student of Kuhn's at Princeton who has authored a series of sophisticated popular works of pro-science partisanship, including frontal assaults on Creationism and socio-biology and a qualified defence of genomic-based eugenics. Most recently, in *Science, Truth and Democracy* (Oxford: Oxford University Press, 2001), Kitcher has turned his hand to the classic Platonic problem of protecting science and society from each other – as opposed to (what I believe is more important) increasing their mutual accountability. Finally, on Kuhn's unwitting ignition of the Science Wars, see Ziauddin Sardar, *Thomas Kuhn and the Science Wars* (Cambridge: Icon Books, 2000).

The various rounds of the *Positivismusstreit* are presented in *The Positivist Dispute in German Sociology*, ed. Theodor Adorno, trans. David Frisby (London: Heinemann, 1976). The similarity of Adorno's and Popper's views on the epistemology and methodology of social research is less apparent from Adorno's debate with Popper than his final set of lectures at the University of Frankfurt (1968–9), which are now transcribed and translated: Theodor Adorno, *Introduction to Sociology*, trans. Edmund Jephcott (Cambridge: Polity Press, 2000). This book is usefully compared with Popper's *The Poverty of Historicism*. Popper's critique of astrology appears in *Conjectures and Refutations*. Adorno's critique – based on the 1952–3 daily astrology column of the *Los Angeles Times* – appears in *The Stars Down to Earth and Other Essays on the Irrational Culture* (London: Routledge, 1998). Interestingly, Karl

Mannheim sets the precedent for Kuhn's 'Planck Effect', that is, the explanation of paradigm change by inter-generational succession – a problem that clearly plagued the *Positivismusstreit*'s reception. The *locus classicus* for this still under-developed area of sociology is Mannheim's 'The Problem of Generations' (1928), republished in his *Essays in the Sociology of Knowledge* (London: Routledge, 1952).

The *locus classicus* for negative responsibility is J.J.C. Smart and Bernard Williams, *Utilitarianism: For and Against* (Cambridge: Cambridge University Press, 1973), pp. 93–100. Williams, as anti-utilitarian, introduces the concept in order to critique it, in favour of a proto-Rortyan ethic of the life-project. Williams' critique focuses on two hypothetical cases that seem inspired by Cold War intrigue, one involving a scientist's decision to engage in weapons research. Some excellent scene-setting for Cold War academia are John McCumber, *Time in the Ditch: American Philosophy in the McCarthy Era* (Evanston: Northwestern University Press, 2001); Philip Mirowski, *Machine Dreams: Economics Becomes a Cyborg Science* (Cambridge: Cambridge University Press, 2001). The problems facing contemporary historians trying to make sense of this period are surveyed in *The Historiography of Contemporary Science and Technology*, ed. Thomas Söderqvist, (Amsterdam: Harwood Academic Publishers, 1997). Kuhn's views on historiography in *The Essential Tension* are usefully compared with Michel Foucault, *Power/Knowledge: Selected Interviews and Other Writings 1972–1977* (Brighton: Harvester, 1980). The laws of Ibanskian sociology are presented in Jon Elster, *Political Psychology* (Cambridge: Cambridge University Press, 1993).

Those interested in my own project of social epistemology should consult my website (http://www.warwick.ac.uk/~sysdt/Index.html) or my books: *Social Epistemology*, second edition (Indiana: Indiana University Press, 2001 [1988]); *Philosophy of Science and Its Discontents*, second edition (New York: Guilford, 1993 [1989]); *Philosophy, Rhetoric and the End of Knowledge*, second edition, with James Collier (Hillsdale: Lawrence Erlbaum Associates, 2003 [1993]); *Science* (Milton Keynes: Open University Press, 1997); *The Governance of Science: Ideology and the Future of the Open Society* (Milton Keynes: Open University Press, 2000); *Knowledge Management Foundations* (Woburn: Butterworth-Heinemann, 2002).

Other science titles available from
Icon Books:

Dawkins vs. Gould

Kim Sterelny

'Book of the Month' – *Focus* magazine

'Slim and readable ... the aficionado of evolutionary theory and the intense debate it engenders would do well to read it.' *Nature*

'A deft little book ... its insights are both useful and fun.' *The Australian*

Science has seen its fair share of punch-ups over the years, but one debate, in the field of biology, has become notorious for its intensity. Over the last twenty years, Richard Dawkins and Stephen Jay Gould have engaged in a savage battle over evolution that shows no sign of waning.

Kim Sterelny moves beyond caricature to expose the *real* differences between the conceptions of evolution of these two leading scientists. He shows that the conflict extends beyond evolution to their very beliefs in science itself; and, in Gould's case, to domains in which science plays no role at all.

ISBN 1-84046-249-3   Paperback   £5.99

The Discovery of the Germ
John Waller

From Hippocrates to Louis Pasteur, the medical profession relied on almost wholly mistaken ideas as to the cause of infectious illness. Bleeding, induced vomiting and mysterious nostrums remained staple remedies. Surgeons, often wearing butcher's aprons caked in surgical detritus, blithely spread infection from patient to patient.

Then came the germ revolution: after two decades of scientific virtuosity, outstanding feats of intellectual courage and bitter personal rivalries, doctors at last realised that infectious diseases are caused by microscopic organisms.

Perhaps the greatest single advance in the history of medical thought, the discovery of the germ led directly to safe surgery, large-scale vaccination programmes, dramatic improvements in hygiene and sanitation, and the pasteurisation of dairy products. Above all, it set the stage for the brilliant emergence of antibiotic medicine to which so many of us now owe our lives.

In this book, John Waller provides a gripping insight into twenty years in the history of medicine that profoundly changed the way we view disease.

ISBN 1-84046-373-2   Hardback   £9.99

An Entertainment for Angels

Patricia Fara

'A concise, lively account.' Jenny Uglow, author of *The Lunar Men* (2002)

'Neat and stylish ... Fara's account of Benjamin Franklin's circle of friends and colleagues brings them squabbling, eureka-ing to life.' *The Guardian*

'Vividly captures the ferment created by the new science of the Enlightenment ... Fara deftly shows how new knowledge emerged from a rich mix of improved technology, medical quackery, Continental theorising, religious doubt and scientific rivalry.' *New Scientist*

'Combines telling anecdote with wise commentary ... presents us with numerous tasty and well-presented historical morsels.' *Times Higher Education Supplement*

Electricity was the scientific fashion of the Enlightenment, 'an Entertainment for Angels, rather than for Men'. Patricia Fara tells the engrossing tale of the strange birth of electrical science – from a high-society party trick to a symbol of man's emerging dominance over nature.

ISBN 1-84046-348-1   Hardback   £9.99

Eureka!

Andrew Gregory

'Marvel as Andrew Gregory explains how the Greeks destroyed myths and gods in favour of a rule-based cosmos ... A readable, pocket-sized primer and a worthwhile present for anyone who needs to fill in the gaps in their knowledge.' *New Scientist*

Eureka! shows that science began with the Greeks. Disciplines as diverse as medicine, biology, engineering, mathematics and cosmology all have their roots in ancient Greece. Plato, Aristotle, Pythagoras, Archimedes and Hippocrates were amongst its stars – master architects all of modern, as well as ancient, science. But what lay behind this colossal eruption of scientific activity?

Free from intellectual and religious dogma, the Greeks rejected explanation in terms of myths and capricious gods, and, in distinguishing between the natural and the supernatural, they were the first to discover nature. New theories began to be developed and tested, leading to a rapid increase in the sophistication of knowledge, and ultimately to an awareness of the distinction between science and technology.

Andrew Gregory unravels the genesis of science in this fascinating exploration of the origins of Western civilisation and our desire for a rational, legitimating system of the universe.

ISBN 1-84046-289-2   Hardback   £9.99

Knowledge is Power

John Henry

Francis Bacon, the renowned English statesman and man of letters, is a leading figure in the history of science. Yet he never made a major discovery, provided a lasting explanation of any physical phenomena or revealed any hidden laws of nature. How then can he rank alongside the likes of Isaac Newton – one of the finest scientists of them all?

Bacon was the first major thinker to describe how science should be done, and to explain why it should be done that way. Against the tide of his times, he rejected the gathering of scientific knowledge for its own sake. Instead, he saw the bounty of science in terms of practical benefit to mankind, and its advance as a means to improve the daily lives of his contemporaries. But foremost, and thus making by far his greatest contribution, Bacon promoted the use of experimentation, coming to outline and define the rigorous procedures of the 'scientific method' that today forms the very bedrock of modern scientific progress.

In this fascinating and accessible book, John Henry gives a dramatic account of the background to Bacon's innovations and the sometimes unconventional sources for his ideas. He explains how magic, civil service bureaucracy and the belief in a forthcoming apocalypse came together in the creation of Bacon's legacy, why he was so concerned to revolutionise the attitude to scientific knowledge – and why his ideas for reform still resonate today.

ISBN 1-84046-356-2   Hardback   £9.99

Latitude & the Magnetic Earth

Stephen Pumfrey

'A chunky read with much more to it than first meets the eye. [Stephen Pumfrey] marshals his scientific and philosophical themes impressively while adding flesh to the hitherto enigmatic Gilbert.' *New Scientist*

'This bijou volume is most valuable for its insights … It is as much for his method as for his conclusions that we should remember this great Elizabethan.' *TLS*

William Gilbert (1544–1603) was royal physician to Queen Elizabeth I and the most distinguished man of science to emerge from her reign. He is the inventor of the term 'electricity', the father of electrical studies, the creator of modern magnetic science and – most famously – the discoverer of the Earth's magnetic nature. Yet, incredibly, he is largely unknown.

Gilbert's close contact with the elite mariners of Elizabethan London enabled him to learn of the magnetic compass and of the strange behaviour of its magnetised needle – a phenomenon known as the magnetic 'dip'. Using a pioneering experimental method, he came to realise that the Earth is a giant magnet; a great body imbued with a 'magnetic soul' that drove it forward in its Copernican orbit. In this golden age of circumnavigations of the globe and of the founding of new colonies, he was the first to use magnetism to determine the latitude of a ship at sea. Alongside these discoveries, Gilbert's writings – some even proposing to solve the problem of longitude – challenged the scientific orthodoxy of his day, and boldly led the battle to establish our modern ideas of terrestrial magnetism.

Lively and accessible, *Latitude & the Magnetic Earth* – the first new exploration of Gilbert for forty years – brings the story up to date, leaving the reader with a vivid feel not only for the conflicts surrounding Gilbert's discoveries and his scientific legacy, but for the man himself.

ISBN 1-84046-290-6   Hardback   £9.99

How Far is Up?

John & Mary Gribbin

How far is it to the edge of the Universe? Less than eighty years ago astronomers began to realise that the Milky Way galaxy in which we live is just one island in an immense ocean of space.

Award-winning authors John and Mary Gribbin tell the story of how the cosmic distance scale was measured, the personalities involved and the increasingly sophisticated instruments they used. Astronomers can now study light from objects so distant that it has taken ten billion years on its journey across space to us, travelling all the time at a speed of 300,000 kilometres per second: that's how far up is!

ISBN 1-84046-439-9   Hardback   £9.99

The Manhattan Project

Jeff Hughes

Established in 1942 at the height of the Second World War, the Manhattan Project was a dramatic quest to beat the Nazis to a deadly goal: the atomic bomb. At Los Alamos and several other sites, American, British, Canadian and refugee European scientists, together with engineers, technicians and many other workers, laboured to design and build nuclear weapons. Their efforts produced 'Little Boy' and 'Fat Man', the bombs that ultimately destroyed Hiroshima and Nagasaki in August 1945.

A vast and secret 'state within a state', the Manhattan Project cost $2 billion. It catapulted scientists – particularly nuclear scientists – to positions of intellectual prestige and political influence. State funds flowed for science as never before, and led to the creation of huge new research institutes, especially large particle accelerators designed to explore the properties of matter – like that at CERN, near Geneva. With their huge experiments, complex organisation and lavish funding, these institutes represented a new form of scientific organisation: 'Big Science'.

Yet, from the large astronomical telescopes of the nineteenth century to the factory-like laboratories of the 1930s, 'Big Science' has a social and scientific history that long pre-dates the advent of the atom bomb. Arguing that the Manhattan Project both drew on and accelerated a trend already well under way, Jeff Hughes offers a lively reinterpretation of the key elements in the history and mythology of twentieth-century science.

ISBN 1-84046-376-7   Hardback   £9.99

Perfect Copy

Nicholas Agar

Cloning represents some of the most exciting – and some of the most morally complex – science of our time.

In 1997 Ian Wilmut and his team announced that they had done the impossible: they had cloned a mammal from an adult cell. This breakthrough prompted immediate calls for the new technology to be used on humans. Italian fertility specialist Severino Antinori hopes to use cloning to give infertile couples the opportunity to at last become parents. Cloning may also solve, once and for all, the problem of rejection that bedevils transplant surgery. Perhaps it even holds the secret of eternal life.

But plans to clone humans have triggered an international storm of protest. Scientists, including Wilmut, politicians from left and right, and theologians from almost all religions find the idea not just unsavoury, but abhorrent.

In this book, Nicholas Agar provides a uniquely accessible exploration of this highly controversial issue. Starting with the biology, and building up the scientific background step by step, *Perfect Copy* provides the perfect guide to the moral labyrinth that surrounds the cloning debate.

ISBN 1-84046-380-5   Paperback   £7.99